Enter Pirates

4

Additional titles by Laurie Notaro

The Idiot Girls' Action-Adventure Club
Autobiography of a Fat Bride
I Love Everybody and Other Atrocious Lies
We Thought You Would Be Prettier
An Idiot Girls' Christmas
There's A Slight Chance I Might Be Going To Hell
The Idiot Girl and the Flaming Tantrum of Death
Spooky Little Girl
It Looked Different on the Model
The Pottymouth at the Table
Housebroken (Summer, 2016)
Crossing the Horizon (Fall, 2016)

A note...

"Hey," my sister Lisa said when I answered the phone. "I'm cleaning out Nana's house and guess what I found?"

"If it's been trapped in that house for the eight years it's been empty and it looks like a leather purse with teeth, I don't want to know," I replied.

"I'll give you a hint," she continued. "It's yellow with age, torn in spots and has your name on it."

"I know," I answered, ashamed. "Apparently, when I stay at Mom's, I leave my underwear all over her house, too. They keep sending it back to me. Dad picks them up with his barbeque tongs."

"I was going to tell you to guess again," my sister said. "But you just grossed me out so bad on the last one that I am going to stop here. Your columns. I found your columns from the State Press."

"You're kidding?" I laughed. "Which ones?"

"All of them," my sister told me. "It looks like every single one. Some of them date back to 1991."

There is a very good possibility that you were not yet born, but I was and working at *The State Press*, the student-run newspaper at Arizona State University. By default, and someone else's drunk driving jail sentence, I ended up writing the humor column mainly because I gave myself the job. I was the editor of the arts and entertainment magazine, my humor columnist was trying to make bail and someone had to fill the spot.

It was an assignment of necessity, and I used to feel embarrassed by it until a world full of bloggers came onto the scene and not only gave themselves their own column, but their own website to boot. At least I was working toward my degree in journalism and had column inches to fill. Yes. JOURNALISM. Now, that word doesn't mean very much, but in 1991, there were several newspapers in every city and you could actually make a living at working at one. Way before the Internet killed that dream, giving birth to not only bloggers but news that doesn't require sources.

Anyway.

I wrote the column, week after week, always hoping to find someone else to do it, but I never did. And 25 years later, I'm still writing it, although newspapers barely exist. I wrote on a Macintosh Classic and barely saved anything on a floppy disk, so unless I had a copy of the magazine itself, most of that stuff was lost to the ages. I never even thought about seeing it again or trying to find copies; I had moved four times since then and whatever made it to my basement in Oregon was undoubtedly dissolved in one of our many sewer overflows.

And then came my sister's phone call. She found a Giorgio Armani bag stuffed full of newspaper stories, my columns that Nana and Pop Pop had clipped out week after week and saved. I couldn't believe it; I thought that stuff was gone forever. My mother mailed it up to Oregon along with Nana's old mink, and honestly, I just let it sit there for a couple of months. While I was curious about seeing my work 25 years later, I was terrified that it would really suck.

And some of them did; there were a couple that were *terrible*. But others weren't half bad, and then several of them actually made me laugh. Although I will admit that I winced at reading some of my own escapades, it was like I had opened my own time capsule and found myself—much younger, thinner, and dumber—inside. There was my world before I had written *Idiot Girls*, before I was married, had nieces and nephews, was still in college and not stopping long enough to even sow my wild oats. I was just dropping them as I went along.

My sister said I should collect them and publish them, sort of a prequel to *Idiot Girls*, and offered to help type them up. My husband also offered to lend his ten fingers, so together, we recreated what I wrote beginning in 1991, and formed a collection I'm calling *Enter Pirates*.

It's not heavy reading, it's goofy and silly and slightly reckless. But it made me laugh, and my biggest hope is that you have the very same reaction.

Awesomely,

Laurie
March 21, 2016

10

Table of Contents

12

Does She Float?

I'm a WITCH!!

If anyone out there has a broom with a V-8 engine and handle bars attached to it, I need to ask you a favor.

See, I'm in some trouble with my five-year-old nephew, Nicholas. It all started innocently enough when he told me that the bully at school, Kevin, had pushed him into the bathroom wall because apparently the ruffian has a princess-sized bladder and had knocked Nicholas out of the way.

I got pretty mad, so I did what any self-respecting aunt would do.

"You tell that boy Kevin that if he EVER pushes you again," I said to my nephew, "Your Aunt Laurie is a witch and she will turn him into a frog boy!"

"Really?" my nephew asked. "You can really do that?"

"Of course, my birthday is on Halloween and Grandma almost named me Tabitha," I stuttered, realizing that the endorsement of black magic and sorcery probably wasn't the best impression I could leave on a tender young mind. "But you know what else I can do that's even WORSE? I'll write a story in the paper about how bad Kevin is at school and then his parents will READ it. And he'll get in big trouble, I bet!"

Extortion, I've found, is always a much better option than voodoo.

"That's dumb," Nicholas replied. "Nobody in my class can read. I like the frog boy idea better."

So it began as a little game that we played, I was Endora and Nicholas was my tiny, inquisitive familiar. To bring it on home, I'd pretend to turn the lights off with my powers while my elbow and the wall switch did the dirty work; I'd offer to read his mind, which wasn't difficult because a) he's five (Pokemon) and b) he's male (Britney Spears); or I'd spook him out by seeing into the future and predicting the ending on a Seinfeld episode I'd already seen 1,000 times. It may not have been the right thing to encourage, but it made the kid feel safe that someone was protecting him when none of his adult peeps was around.

His doubt, however, began to surface. "If you're a witch," he asked me one afternoon when we went to see a movie and were waiting for it to start, "Why did we drive over here? Why didn't we ride your broom?"

"Dude!" I said, as my mind raced with a worthy answer. "It's still NINETY-ONE degrees outside! My broom doesn't have air conditioning!"

"I don't think I believe you're really a witch," he said. "My daddy says you're 'troubled' and you need to go back to the doctor."

I put my fingers to my temple. "Mmmmmmmm," I hummed. "You wish you were playing Pokeman with Britney Spears!"

"Hmmmph!" my nephew huffed, clearly stumped. "So if you're really a witch, make the lights go off."

"Last night, I had traffic light witch duty, and do you know how exhausting that is? Red, green, yellow! Red, green, yellow, sometimes they throw in an arrow, and it never stops!" I commented. "Frankly, I'm tired. If you want the lights out, do it yourself."

Nicholas put his fingers to his temples, and then mumbled, "Lights, go out!"

And they did. My nephew gasped with excitement, and I choked back my surprise.

He closed his eyes, took a moment then said, "Movie, start now!"

Suddenly, the movie started.

When Nicholas opened his eyes, he was astonished, and truthfully, so was I.

"Looks like you have a little bit of witch in you," I whispered.

But the magic wasn't over yet.

I was at work the following Monday afternoon when my mother called.

"Hey, wacko!" my mother started. "Today, Nicholas said, 'Guess what, Grandma? I'm a warlock!' He also told his whole class that when it gets cooler, his aunt will bring her witch broom to school and everyone can ride it. They all think he's Harry Potter! Now you'll know what it feels like to get blamed for somebody's mental defects! Either you wiggle your nose and get a broom that levitates or start saving up for his therapy!"

"Oh no," I moaned. "I never meant for this to happen! I guess I'm going to have to pick up a couple extra shifts of traffic light duty."

HELLO. GOODBYE.

It was kind of like waiting to go to the gas chamber.

I knew it was coming, but I didn't know when, and I knew I wasn't going to like it.

And I was completely and utterly powerless to do anything about it.

The plug was about to be pulled on my phone, my umbilical cord, my extension to the outside world and one of my favorite reasons for living.

I had been notified of this, receiving threats in the mail for the past four weeks. Initially, the phone company was sympathetic. The first threat was simply a reminder, because, as they put it, they understood that sometimes bills are overlooked and forgotten. It was a kind and warm letter, I smiled when I read it. It seemed so, well, *caring*.

The second notice, however, took on a slightly different tone, and they let me know, in not so many words, that the phone company was a little pissed at me. In other words, *Shame On Laurie* for not paying her bill.

In the third letter, it was apparent that our relationship had suffered and would continue to degenerate until I had coughed up the balance due, and I found that quite selfish and absolutely one-sided. I immediately mangled the letter and threw it in the trash. Who did they think they were talking to, I screamed. They were not the boss of me!

When I was served with the fourth and final letter, however, the phone company announced that they wanted a divorce. I cried. I was stunned that they could be so cruel after we had spent so many quality years together.

Everyday after that last letter, the first thing I did when the sun went down and I woke up, aside from reaching for a cigarette, was check to see if the phone still had a pulse. And for five days, the phone rang and gurgled, hummed and laughed, and we both lived each day as if there were no tomorrows.

On the fifth day, however, when I reached for the phone, it's touch was stiff and cold. I picked up the reciever in an action of denial, positive that I would hear that familiar and loving tone, but only silence filled my ears. The only way I can describe it is that the world exploded and froze in the same instant.

My baby fell from my hands to the floor. It was dead.

"You bastards!" I cried in a scream that left my body and went shrieking through the air, my hand in a fist, shaking towards the sky, "How could you do this? How could God allow this to happen?"

I shrunk to the floor, my head in my hands, and I wept.

I wept for the phone, I wept for myself, I wept for all the people that I needed to call to inform them that I no longer could call them. I no longer had a phone, I no longer had a phone number, I no longer had an identity, I no longer had a soul.

I had become NOTHING.

I panicked. I ran to my sister's house in my hour of need and pounded on the door. When she saw me, she collected the shell of a human being that I had been reduced to and took me inside.

"What happened?" she asked me, but I could say nothing, all I could do was shake my head.

"Did you get stood up again?" she said, handing me a tissue to blow my nose.

I shook my head.

"Did someone tell you you were fat?"

I shook my head.

"Did Mom and Dad cut you off monetarily?"

I shook my head.

"Did your boyfriend get another girl pregnant?"

I shook my head.

"Did he get sentenced to prison?"

"No," I sobbed, "That's next week."

"Are you upset about turning 29, spending twelve years in college and still not having a degree, being a drunk and so financially irresponsible that no bank will allow you to have a checking account?"

"No!" I countered. "My phone got shut off!"

"Oh. Well maybe you should get a --"

"*Do not* say that filthy word to me, do not," I said to her, holding my finger up. "Just because you have one doesn't mean that I have to have one, too. Don't even say it."

She looked at me for a second, her brow furrowed, she was thinking about it, I could tell, she was contemplating it, she was forming it and then she did it, it just flew from her mouth like a rabid bat.

"Get a JOB!"

The word echoed through the house like a gunshot, it bounced off each wall, hit me in the head and then fell in my lap.

"I can't believe you did that," I mumbled, still dizzy from the assault. "I never knew you could be so vile and wicked."

"If you got one, maybe you could get cable," my sister tempted, and for a moment, she must must have seen my eyes spring forth, because then she added, "And you could also buy *food!*"

I want cable, a little voice in my head sang, cable is the most beautiful thing in the world besides whiskey. I used to have cable, a long, long time ago before the cable company also divorced me and ripped the wires out of my TV set right before my eyes. To this day, I'm *still* having nightmares about it as well as panic attacks whenever I come in contact with any man in a blue jumper that rings my doorbell.

"So let me get this straight," I said to my sister. "You think if I get one of those 'things' that I could get my phone back, I could get cable and also eat?"

She nodded with a smile.

"So I could watch TV, get drunk, eat Ding Dongs and talk on the phone all day?"

"Not really," she added. "You would have
to spend the daytime at work."

"Oh, I don't like that," I informed her, and decided that I would have to ask my friend Patti for advice.

I found him on the porch at Long Wong's, splitting a pitcher of beer with my other friend, Jeff. They both jumped up when they saw me.

"We thought you were dead!" Patti exclaimed. "Your phone got disconnected."

"I know," I answered. "My sister thinks that if I got a jay-oh-bee that I could get it back."

"Oh my God," Jeff muttered.

Patti, on the other hand, had begun to scream, much like he would if he was exposed to the sun, his lily-white skin soaking up the rays and transforming him into a brittle stick of charcoal in a matter of mere and isolated seconds.

"Calm down," I assured him. "Nothing is definite yet."

"You could do a million things besides get one of those," Jeff proclaimed. "You could have a baby and sell it!"

"You could stand outside of Circle K and beg for change like those hippie kids do," Patti suggested.

"That wouldn't work," I answered. "They all drive nicer cars than I do."

"Sell your hair to the wig factory people," Jeff threw in.

"Yeah, I could do that," I agreed, "But I hate shaving my legs."

"Wait," Patti said, a proud smile expanding over his face, "I know how you can make a ton of money!"

I could tell that he was about to become my savior with the brilliant miracle that was bubbling inside his brain. As I waited silently for his answer, I heard my phone ringing from a distance like a child crying out in despair for its mother. My salvation was seconds away, I almost had my baby back, I was that close.

"Phone sex!"

I heard my baby scream.

The One From Fifth Grade

Remember that girl in fifth grade that was the last one left standing after the blonde and tan captains picked their teams for volleyball? Remember how her inner thighs rubbed together even then, or when the school nurse asked a roomful of ten-year-old girls what men-strooation was when the "womanhood" speech was delivered and only one girl raised her hand because she was *born* with pubic hair? Remember that girl who had pimples when the other girls were still washing their hair with No More Tears, or the one who got braces and always had food stuck in them, the girl who if you ever became friends with her, even the slightest bit, you could never shake her because she followed you everywhere?

Ever wonder about what happened to her?

Well, I do, and I was wondering about that girl as I was waiting for my friend Nikki to finish her waitressing shift last night. I had been stood up by a boy I liked again, thinking that things certainly could be worse. Yeah, okay, this was the fourth time he stood me up, and yeah, I frequent certain bars to such an extent that one bouncer told me he was going to start charging me rent, and yeah, I had a stress-induced boil festering on the side of my face that had taken on the proportions of a tumor more than anything ever concieved by acne, but things could be worse. Sitting at a bar with fellow drunks is seldom considered a group activity, so there was no chance of my being left alone on one side while the rest of the patrons divvied up into teams for an inebriation/vomit challenge. I probably would have been the first one picked, anyway.

"What are you doing here?" Nikki said when she spotted me. "I thought you had a date."

"So did Delta Dawn," I answered. "Why is it that I can equate any situation in my life to an extinct ballad of the '70s?"

"So you're free tonight?" she asked.

"I'm as free as a bird now," I answered. "But this bird you cannot change."

"Well, let's go out then," she said. "Wanna get drunk?"

"I've got enough money on me for two drinks," I explained. "And that's not getting drunk. That's getting teased."

Nikki nodded. "What about dancing? We've never gone out dancing."

"And there's a reason for that," I answered. "The last time I danced, I was in seventh grade. I wasn't physically fit enough to do it without having an asthma attack, and I didn't even smoke then. If I went out dancing now, we'd either have to bring along an oxygen tent or a team of paramedics."

I only went to one school dance anyway, and it was so horrifying that I couldn't bring myself to engage in another. I found myself swaying beneath a glittering disco ball to "Dancing Queen" in the school lunchroom in 1977 with the only boy who ever asked me to dance, a boy so short I rested my chin on the top of his head. He was a boy I knew from science class who once ate the retina from a cow's eyeball that we were supposed to be dissecting. Everyone in the class bet him a dollar to eat it, and when he collected all of the money, he picked up the retina and swallowed it, formaldehyde and all, but he had made thirty bucks in three minutes. *An entrepreneur,* my mother would say, *a good trait in a man.* Then, five minutes later, our teacher found out about it, made him give the money back and dragged him to the nurse who made him puke until she found the eyeball thing. His fame was indeed fast lived, but that didn't prevent him from groping at my seventh grade butt through my purple Dittoes as ABBA glided through that last desperate verse. It was okay, my ass hadn't fallen yet, since that didn't happen until I was a junior in high school.

My dancing story, however, can in no way compare to that of my friend Jamie's, who, at the same dance, was haunted by another short boy who had bathed himself that evening in a boiling vat of Brut and had smoked several cigars, judging by his aroma. He chased her all night, *all night,* until he begged her so shamefully when "Stairway to Heaven" was playing that she considered it charity and said okay. He held her tight. She held her breath. He nestled his greasy little cigar head on her shoulder. She spotted his dandruff. Then he popped a boner. It was a very long song.

Even to this day, *fifteen years later,* if "Stairway to Heaven" comes on the radio, she gets these red splotchy things all over her neck and face and will do whatever it takes to turn the song off. I believe that incident really scarred her, probably for life. "I can't help it," she explained to me once after ripping the cord from a jukebox out of the wall of a bar. "As soon as I hear those first little notes, that smell of Brut and cigars fill my nose; I get real dizzy and hot, and I start feeling a hard little thing, the size of a cocktail frank or Li'l Smokie, rubbing itself all over my leg. I have flashbacks in which my hair is feathered and I'm wearing Earth Shoes."

So, by those accounts, you can see why Nikki's proposal of dancing the night away was, quite obviously, out of the question.

"Okay," Nikki sighed. "How about a movie?"

"No," I responded. "I've seen everything."

"You can't have seen *everything*," she said. "The theater across the street has ten different movies."

"I know," I agreed. "But on Tuesday I was bored, so I paid for one movie and watched it, and I was still bored so I snuck into the other nine and watched them. I didn't come out until midnight."

"Well, if you've already seen everything, then let's rent something."

"I can't," I explained. "I owe the movie rental place eighty dollars because I had that one Madonna movie for two months. I'm afraid that if I so much as walk in the place, I'll end up surrounded by a SWAT team; they're so mad at me."

"You didn't rewind, did you?"

"Who has time to rewind? I didn't even watch all of it. As soon as Harvey Keitel popped up naked, I shut the thing off."

"Maybe I'll just go home," Nikki said, exasperated.

"Yeah, me too," I sighed. "I can pick at this zit and then crank call my mom."

So I left the bar, Nikki went home and I got in my car.

It was on the freeway that I started thinking about that girl again, the one from fifth grade, how she used to hum that song "I Honestly Love You," and convinced herself that if she could just sing that song at a talent show and sing it good, that maybe everyone would like her. It was a bad idea, because I know that the music teacher told her point blank that she was *not* a singer and that she should just stick with what she was good at, which was reading and English, and not embarass herself in front of a crowd of people. I remembered that I kind of hated her, that she always wore the same clothes as me and that she was in every class I had. Everyone always confused the two of us.

I wondered where she was now, what trailer park she lives in, and if she married a custodian or a really dumb criminal. Or maybe what happened to her was that she got a lot of tattoos, started drinking whiskey straight out of the bottle, joined L7 and regrets the times when she didn't kick the shit out of the blonde girls that never picked her for their volleyball teams.

I was hoping, anyway, that that's what happened to her.

I love to see perfect, pretty girls bleed.

And, I have this feeling, an undeniable feeling, that she still gets stood up a lot, too.

Even, maybe, four times in a row.

She was probably driving on the freeway at that very moment, just like I was, smoking a cigartette with all the windows rolled down and the radio turned up, remembering the kid she used to be in fifth grade and trying even harder to forget about it.

Together Together

I needed a vacation.

I needed one badly.

My friend Sandra needed a vacation, too, so one day we called her travel agent, and before we knew it, we were booked on a flight to San Francisco for the following week.

What we did not know, however, was that we were flying the MacFrugal's airline, one that is so discounted and wholesale that the planes don't even have names on them, they're just plain white with a black stripe running down the middle.

We got to the gate a little late, just a little, and tried to get our seating assignments, but right as Sandra was ready to tell the hostess, Bunny, that we wanted a window seat, the woman threw two yellow pieces of plastic at us. We looked at them.

One was numbered 117, and the other was numbered 118. I didn't know what they were for, if we had just been enrolled in some sort of raffle or if we actually weren't at the airline counter at all, but a deli meat counter by mistake.

"I'll take a tub of potato salad and a half-pound of olive loaf," I said to the hostess. "And Sandra would like a ham and cheese hoagie with chips, cause she's a little hungry now."

Bunny didn't think I was being very funny at all, and turned her blonde little head to announce to the rest of the passengers that the flight would begin boarding with numbers one through fifteen immediately.

Oh no, I thought to myself, trying not to alarm Sandra, I know what this means. 117 and 118. By the time they call us, we'll be lucky if we manage to get on the plane by running along side of it during take-off and flinging ourselves onto a wing. That meant no seat belts or little snack trays, but at least I would be able to smoke.

I was a little apprehensive about flying anyway, since the last time I went to San

Francisco, we hit what we thought was a big air pocket until the pilot nonchalantly announced that we might encounter some turbulence, since one of the engines had basically fallen off the plane and was now plummeting at a furious speed towards Las Vegas, where it was destined to become a new headpiece for some showgirl. It was at that point that I started figuring out all of my brownie points for heaven, because I wasn't bound to this world for very much longer, and that was when I understood my eternity, because I heard the Devil laugh. My boyfriend at the time grabbed my hand, but I pushed it away and started digging through my purse. I'd be damned if I only had thirty seconds to live and I didn't go down without a cigarette in my mouth, to hell with the sentimental bullshit.

But believe it or not, Sandra and I walked on the plane like everyone else when numbers 112 plus infinity were called, except that everyone on that flight got on before us. All illusions of window seats or aisle seats were vastly abolished when we realized that we not only wouldn't even get to sit together, but that flying on two-for-one tickets meant exactly that, since it looked like I was going to ride to San Francisco on Sandra's lap. It was slim pickins, to say the least.

Sandra managed to squeeze herself next to a couple with a screaming baby, and I basically sat on the pilot's leg, right next to

Bunny, who was going to be our maid for the flight.

With every seat on the flight occupied, crammed and overflowing, I looked down the aisle and realized I wasn't flying on a plane. I had never been on a plane like this. I was flying on what could only be described as a Vietnamese rickshaw bus gone airborne, and I desperately waited for some flying chickens or a couple of pigs to come snorting down the aisle as Bunny passed out our native bamboo UFO hats.

After we took off, Bunny got up and I hoped that it was snack time, and when I saw her bring a basket back, I knew I was right. Snack Time! I was praying it would be a little sandwich with some fruit and a brownie for dessert, but imagine my surprize when Bunny started whipping out little bags of peanuts and throwing them at people, and if you didn't catch one, you just didn't get to eat. It was as simple as that. I had to wrestle Frieda, the lady sitting across from me who was pretty strong for someone recovering from bypass surgery, for a bag, but when she realized that they were salted, she forked them over because she said she had high blood pressure and couldn't eat them anyway. I got lucky when the second course of our meal came around, Rold Gold pretzels, because Bunny threw them right at the man next to me who had just had a stroke, and I successfully snatched them out of his lap because I was quicker than he was and also that he was shaking so bad that he kept missing them.

After Snack Time, there weren't any magazines to read, except for the one Harper's Bazaar that was so old it had Cheryl Tiegs on the cover, so instead I talked to Frieda, who couldn't understand why I didn't ever want a job, and then I picked through some of my dreads, pulled out the dead hair and then rolled them into little balls.

When we finally landed, Sandra and I were glad, and we grabbed our shit and headed out to find the Super Shuttle that was going to take us to my friend Gavi's house, where we we staying. We found the shuttle without too many problems, told the driver where we wanted to go and he happily loaded up our stuff. We were already in the van when a mean man with a walkie-talkie came along and grabbed my arm and pulled us out of the van, then started throwing all of our bags into the street. He kicked us off of the Super Shuttle, started screaming that "Cheating is not tolerated on the Super Shuttle! You cannot cheat!" and punished us by sending Sandra and I to the end of the very long Super Shuttle line which was invisible when we first walked up.

Apparently, we took cuts when we weren't supposed to, and we stood at the back of the line feeling pretty dumb, especially when the mean shuttle man kept looking at us and shaking his head. I got in trouble again when a man in front of us got on the shuttle and forgot his jacket on the railing, so Sandra and I were trying to do the polite San Francisco thing, shouting, "Sir! Sir! You forgot your jacket!" We were trying to throw it to him just as the mean shuttle man marched up again, ripped the jacket from our hands, sighed, put his hand on his hip and informed us that the jacket was *his* and if we wanted a ride *anywhere,* we probably shouldn't try and give it away to ANY OTHER PEOPLE.

Eventually, we got to Gavi's and we saw lots of San Francisco treats, mainly because Gavi lives 500 feet from a housing project. We got to see people smoking lots of crack, prostitutes, and folks shooting off guns. We saw one man throwing rocks at the next door neighbor's window, and he finally threw enough of them that someone opened the window and threw back a big package, which he stuck in his pants, and we also got to see a lady get another package, only she stuck it in her baby's diaper. The most amazing thing we saw at Gavi's house, however, was a girl who walked down the street, pulled a hammer from her pocket and bashed in a car windshield until it had a hole in it and then she put the hammer back in her pocket and walked away. Nobody said or did anything, especially not us, except for the neighbor across the street who hauled down all of his knives and swords and began sharpening them on his front steps.

The best thing about San Francisco is that everyone thought that Sandra and I were *together* together, like girlfriend/girlfriend, and that was fine with us, because we liked hanging with the sisters, they hate men more than I do. We even met these two sailors on leave that told us that they knew right away that we were lesbians, and we didn't try to prove them wrong, no we didn't. They also said that Sandra was obviously the dominant one, so she was the husband and that I was the wife.

I liked that part, too.

They usually always peg me for the husband.

Enter Pirates

It was only a rib.

Jim had already taken advantage of seven of them with the all-you-can-eat platter, and the eighth one simply wasn't going down.

It rested alone on the dish, the lone survivor of a mad eating rampage, the results of which sat on an opposing plate, white, shiny and gnawed.

The last rib bothered Jim.

He looked at it.

He touched it a little, toyed with the idea of perhaps taking just one bite so that leaving it on the plate untouched wouldn't seem so wasteful.

He looked at me.

"Should I eat it?" he questioned.

I shrugged.

"I really can't. I mean really. *I can't.*"

I nodded.

"I can't just leave it here, it's a perfectly good rib."

"I know," I agreed. "But what are you going to do with *one* rib? Nobody ever ate just *one* rib. It's only *one* rib. That's why they have it listed in plural on the menu. Rib-*ssss.*"

"It would make a good weapon," he said, thinking. "Or I could dig holes with it."

"Why just take that one, then?" I responded. "Let's bag all of the bones, pick up some cinder blocks and couple of milk crates on the way home and you can build yourself a mortal remains entertainment center with them."

He ignored me.

"I have a feeling about this rib," he said. "This rib is special. Don't ask me to explain it. I can't. It's just a feeling."

"My God, Jim, it's a rib!" I argued. "Don't tell me you see the image of a savoir in it!"

He looked at the rib closely, rather studied it, and then looked at me.

"No, it's not Jesus," he whispered. "But this rib is . . . . . .*holy*. I'm telling you, it has a purpose."

"All right, Jim, if you say so," I gave in. "When the waiter comes back around, ask him if he can wrap it up in the Shroud of Turin instead of a sheet of tin foil."

After we had The Rib, as it became known, wrapped, blessed and anointed, we headed towards our friend Dave's house to see if his girlfriend would let him out of the house for the night.

We had one problem, though. Dave's girlfriend hated us. She hated us a lot. More than that. In fact, I think it would be a fair statement to say that Dave's girlfriend SuperHated us, maybe even to the point of *loathing*.

Apparently, she hated Jim and me for a variety of reasons, which included but were not limited to, the fact that Dave liked us, the fact that Dave had fun with us, the fact that we had senses of humor and that she had never gotten around to purchasing one. She hated us because she thought that we made Dave drink, although it is a well-known fact that he never needed any general prodding in that area. As a matter of fact, at the last party Jim had, Dave vaporized forty-five minutes after he arrived and after consuming a fifth of Jack Daniel's in that time period, by himself. Jim found him in the gravel in front of the apartment, entirely unconscious, and as he described it, Dave was "laying on his side and looking like a deer that had been hit by a large car, maybe a Lincoln," since all four of his appendages were parallel to each other in 90 degree angles from his body. He also had a pool of vomit streaming from his mouth, and he was real sweaty. For the remainder of the night, Dave's activities were confined to vomiting into the pot that Jim usually boils potatoes in.

In any case, she hated us, but she hated me more than Jim because, well, I'm a chick and she's a chick, and chicks hate other chicks just because they're chicks, I guess. She actually hated me more that a regular chick, because I was a *single* chick.

Dave's girlfriend didn't take too kindly to the fact that the three of us were spending time together, and Jim and I felt bad about this, because we both liked her. She made great dips and always served an unrivaled fruit platter when she and Dave had parties. We tried to be nice to her, but she would still have no part of us, not even when I told her that she looked *thin*.

Then, one night, Jim and I won a pink Playboy Bunny sticker in a gumball machine and figured that Dave's mailbox was as good of a place as any to put it on, and also kinda because we thought it might piss his girlfriend off a little. However, the next day, Dave told us that his girlfriend thought it was funny and actually chuckled at it.

Naturally, Jim and I thought we were accomplishing great strides in the effort to make her like us, and that she might give Dave permission to spend more time than just one night a week with us. This was a good thing, since our duties as Dave's Bad Influences not only required dragging him through the seedy underbelly of alcoholism, but we also had plans to hold him down and make him smoke crack until he was an addict and then we were going to pimp him out so we could, in turn, buy more drugs. You see, we needed to influence Dave *at least* twice a week.

So, to us, it seemed like the right thing to do that night after we had eaten dinner to bring his girlfriend an offering. Jim and I dug through the trash in the car only to come up with 217 cigarette butts from the ashtray and three decomposing meatballs from underneath the passenger seat that my Nana had given me two weeks before but that I forgot about. Neither of them felt very friendly, and we were stumped until we spied the hallowed remnant of Jim's all-you-can-eat-special.

The Rib.

It was perfect.

"Oh my God," I said to Jim excitedly. *"Enter Pirates!"*

He looked at me and didn't say anything.

"Enter Pirates!" I said again, almost shouting.

I had a Shakespeare class the year before and we read *Pericles*, which is a play about a very happy king and his queen, a shipwreck, and the play is going along very nicely and then the stage directions say, "Enter Pirates." Just like that. No warning, so forehadowing, all of a sudden...pirates. And life is like that, I explained to Jim as we drove over to Dave's house, *"Enter Pirates!"* One minute your life is plodding along on its path, and then the next thing you know, there's a tickly beard in your ear and a sword at your throat.

Or a rib in your mailbox.

We knew it was perfect as we quietly slipped it into the mailbox, and we were so happy with ourselves that we couldn't help but giggle a little when we knocked on the door and Dave answered it.

Dave, on the other hand, didn't look so happy. His face was all red, his shirt was half-untucked and he had little beads of sweat on his forehead and above his upper lip.

Dave looked like he was drunk.

Dave looked like hell.

Dave was in TROUBLE.

"She's not going to work tonight," he told us. "She wants to stay home and fight. I think I'm grounded."

"What are you fighting about?" we asked.

He laughed. "Well, it was all about what a bastard I was before," he said. "But I'm sure when I go back in the ring, it will now be about you guys."

The following day, neither of us heard from Dave, and far be it from me and Jim to stir up the hornet's nest, so we decided to lay low until Dave made contact with us. We knew he was so far in the doghouse that she had probably nailed the bathroom door shut and was making him shit in the grass.

Finally, several days later, Dave was able to spring himself from the house unnoticed long enough to make contact to us via a pay phone. That was a good sign, since we had expected that Dave would only be able to communicate through messenger birds, using leaves for paper and his blood for ink. We made arrangements to meet for drinks later that night and talk about what happened with the Ball and Chain.

But when I saw him sitting at the bar I didn't expect him to be in the shape he was in. There he was, a shot of whiskey in one hand and a lit Marlboro in the other, his face robust and rich, his eyes *alive*. He was smiling. He was giddy. I had never seen him so happy. I seriously doubt that I'll ever see him that happy again until the day he gets off parole and he gets his civil rights reinstated.

"Dave, you look like a new man," Jim and I agreed.

"Are you kidding? *Claus von Bulow* never felt this happy," Dave smiled.

"Can you tell us what happened?" we asked.

"Well, after you left, we actually worked a lot of things out," he said. "She decided that I needed to be more attentive and to recognize her feelings, and I decided I was going to start lacing her food with Prozac.

"So everything was going along fine, she even stopped talking long enough at one point that I caught a fifteen-minute nap.

"And then she found The Rib."

My stomach and lower intestines felt like I had been eating Pop Rocks and drinking Pepsi,

48

which is what I believe *really* killed River Phoenix.

Dave relayed the sequence of events this way:

Apparently, Dave's neighbor across the street was quite fond of beating the hell out of his wife, and several nights before, one of the other neighbors called the police. As the Wife-Beating neighbor was being arrested and shoved in the back seat of the patrol car, he spotted Dave's girlfriend, who was watching the commotion and being nosey, and screamed to her that he was going to get her for calling the cops on him.

So when she went to the mailbox that fateful morning and found The Rib, she somehow equated this to the threat and became convinced that The Rib had become a symbol of her death at the hands of the Wife-Beating neighbor. She became very excited and adamant about calling the police because the neighbor had left a body part in her mailbox, "just like the Mafia does," and that The Rib needed to be dusted for fingerprints as proof.

Dave looked at The Rib and knew immediately that it was the work of myself and Jim, and in a feeble attempt to calm her down, he told her this.

In a boomerang turn of events, Dave's girlfriend became even *more* agitated and began screaming *louder* that he*"needed to make friends

*with a better class of people,'" that "It's time that girl
realized she's almost thirty,"* and *"I bet they were
drunk or spaced-out on drugs when they did it."*

Or, in other words, *Enter Pirates.*

"I am *not* almost thirty," I said through
clenched teeth when Dave was finished.

"And what did you say, Dave?" Jim
ventured.

"I said, *'I'm moving out,'* and then I called
U-Haul," Dave answered.

"I have a *year-and-a-half* before I'm thirty,"
I protested.

"God, Dave, I'm sorry," Jim said, shaking
his head.

"Naw, it's okay. I should have just told
her that The Rib is an old family tradition. 'You
see, you put a dime in the mailbox every day for
a month, and on the last day, The Rib Fairy
brings you a rib. *And now,* because *she's* not a
family member and *she* touched the rib, it's all
ruined and that *I've* got to start my cycle all over
again!'"

"I'm sorry, Dave," I said. "We never
wanted you guys to split up."

"No, we never wanted you guys to break
up," Jim agreed.

"Actually, we did," I confessed.

"Yeah, we did," Jim nodded.

"Her dips weren't *that* good," I
mentioned.

"Well, I *did* like the caramel fondue stuff she made for those apples," Jim threw in. "It was so creamy."

"She bought it pre-made at the store," Dave offered. "It's in the produce section."

Jim gasped.

"This whole time, if I just could have known that all it was going to take was a rib, I would have sent you guys to Sizzler long ago," Dave reflected. "I might have even paid for the dinner."

"I didn't know," I agreed. "It was only a rib. Who knew?"

"I knew," Jim noted. "I told you that rib was holy."

"So whatever happened to The Rib?" I asked. "Did you eat it?"

"No, she threw it away when she realized she didn't need it for evidence," Dave answered. "It was only *one* rib. Nobody eats just *one* rib."

"True," we agreed.

Sometimes, though, one rib is more than enough.

Everything's Bigger in Texas, Part One

I've never had good timing.

    I didn't have it before I shattered my knee in sixth grade a week before my class went on a field trip to the zoo, and instead of walking around to see the animals like the other kids, my mom had to push me in a wheelchair; I didn't have it when I had an allergic reaction to hair dye in which my head and face swelled to such proportions that I looked like the Elephant Man, on the same day my ex-boyfriend got busted for drugs while driving a U-Haul full of my furniture while were moving into a new house; and I *especially* didn't have it two weeks ago when I paid off most of my cable bill with money I borrowed from my mom, although at precisely the same moment, the bastards were snipping the wires and disconnected me for non-payment.

    So I should have known, it must have become obvious at some point, that when Troy made the airline reservations for our trip to South by Southwest in Austin, *something* was going to go horribly, horribly wrong.

Tragedy chose to unveil itself two days before the trip when a disc in my lower back decided to unlodge itself in search of finer accomodations. As it went floating around my kidneys and intestines for a new happenin' place to live, the big nerve in my spine got pinched and made me paralyzed and pretty much crippled.

This made traveling *anywhere,* even to the bathroom, a carnival of pain. I stayed in bed for the next two days, but by the time that the day came for us to leave, I was still in really bad shape. Friends dug through their bathroom cabinets and pockets for extra pain killers to help me. My boyfriend told me to "just stay as drunk as you can" for the next five days.

Troy tried to helped me out by carrying all of my luggage in addtion to his, through the airport and onto the plane. I was helpless. I felt like my Aunt Margaret, who had crippled herself several years ago in a bizarre baking accident because she was drinking gin and making a cake at the same time. In a drunken tumble, she slipped on some flour she had spilled on the floor and got crushed when a wrought-iron kitchen chair fell on top of her.

Anyway, the plane ride wasn't so bad since I got to sit down, and it got even better when our friendly steward, Rodney, brought me a stiff Bloody Mary at exactly 7:15 a.m.

A couple of hours later, we were landing in Austin, which, to all of you who don't already know, is a Clean-Air City. What this means, we found out later, was that smoking is politely discouraged by installing restrictions on where and when you can do it. For example, as Troy and I were trying to catch a cab to our hotel, the only place we were allowed to light up was outside on a sidewalk, in between two red arrows strategically painted on the side of the terminal.

We finally got the attention of a cab driver who drove us to the hotel, but not before he mentioned that a) the population of Austin, Texas was in between 25 and 600,000, and b) the next time he won the lottery, (he had already captured a $22 winning ticket) he was going to buy himself a woman.

"Yeah," Troy mentioned. "You'd be amazed at what you can get for 22 bucks these days."

The first thing that Troy and I did when we got to the hotel room was throw ourselves on each of the double beds in the room, and then Troy looked over and smiled wildly.

"You're sleeping with Charlie," he said smugly.

The other half of our traveling group, Charlie and Laura, weren't due to arrive until later that night.

"No way," I said. "We're sleeping girl/girl in one bed and boy/boy in the other, just like at camp."

"That's what you think," he said as his smile faded. "Charlie farts more in his sleep than he does when he's awake."

Troy oughta know. He lived with Charlie, a man who keeps wearing his underwear until the waistband stretches out so far he has to keep them up with safety pins, for eight months. It was kinda true, anyway. Every time a foul smelled drifted into the *Planet* office, all fingers always pointed to Charlie.

"That's right, that's right," Charlie protested one day. "They always blame the Fat Guy. Whenever anything stinks, the Fat Guy farted. Anytime somebody's food is missing, the Fat Guy ate it. It's always the fault of the Fat Guy."

So by the time that our other half arrived, it had been decided. Laura was sleeping with me. Troy was sleeping alone. The Fat Guy was sleeping on the floor. It wasn't that bad. We threw him all of our extra blankets. Charlie was in a bad mood, anyway, since Laura told us that he had been so "overzealous" on the plane that he bugged the remaining passengers on the flight so efficiently that the woman next to him snapped at him, calling him "Fat Boy."

The next day, Troy, Laura and I felt kinda bad about making Charlie sleep on a brown shag rug, so we ordered him a roll-away bed from the front desk. When it came to the room, we decided to suprise him and get it all set up before he came back from his jog. Well, Laura and Troy actually did. I was still immobile in bed.

That was when we discovered it. Charlie, although he had been in Texas for barely 18 hours, had already created a habitat of sorts for himself in a corner of the room. Tucked and hidden in his circular mound of blankets were saltine crackers, peanuts, little bits of cookie, a varied assortment of magazines and every article of clothing he had brought from Tempe. Charlie had built himself a NEST. The curiosity of it was enough to force me to get up and hobble over and poke at it. I had never seen any other human being familiarize themselves with anything the way Charlie had. It seemed so . . . well, *feral*. I wished I had some lint from my dryer to offer him, or little bits of string.

When Charlie came back from his jog with two big bags of food in his hands, however, he wasn't pleased at all. Not one bit.

"What's this for?" he asked. "Why'd you guys move my stuff?"

"Oh, that's right," Troy said dryly to Charlie. "We'd forgotten that you didn't know what a bed looked like, *Nell.*"

So it was decided that Laura would now sleep on the roll away, and Charlie moved his nest in front of the dresser, which, naturally, blocked our path to anything.

That night, I downed half of the pain killers I had in my possesion, Troy bought me a lot of drinks and I was able to walk. We headed out for a night on the Texas town. We needed to get to the other side of the university, and I sure as hell couldn't walk it, so we made a Tempe, Arizona attempt at hailing a cab, which, according to Charlie, involved standing in the middle of the street, wildly flapping his arms, jumping up and down and yelling until a cab stopped or just plain ran into him.

The cab driver that pulled up to us seemed normal enough, he was cheery, accommodating and told us directly that at the last census taken, the population of Austin rolled in at right about 450,000. His name was Jack Allen, no relation to Steve Allen, although "I do come from a musical family," he assurred us.

While Jack Allen was explaining this, we all saw it, there was no way to ignore it. It stunned everybody in the cab, we all succumbed to a sudden state of silence.

We all said to ourselves, "Be quiet, don't mention it, mind your own business," that is, each of us had said that to ourselves but me.

Well, it wasn't really me, but the pills and whiskey that was running like a river through my bloodstream that leaned forward and pointed, exclaiming, "Jack Allen, those are the biggest hands I have EVER SEEN."

Secretly, I think Jack Allen was just waiting for us to notice. He was suprised that no one had pointed it out sooner. You could tell this by the way he lifted his fingers, each the size and thickness of a bloated bratwurst, so delicately, as if each of his hands didn't weigh as much as a Butterball turkey waiting to feed an extended family numbering well into double digits.

Jack Allen's hands weren't BIG. They weren't HUGE. They weren't even GARGANTUAN. The only fair way to describe the enormity of Jack Allen's hands were to say they were CIRCUS SIZE.

He was pleased that we had discovered his attribute, and he smiled broadly.

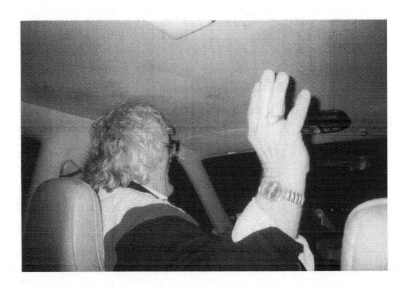

"See this ring?" Jack Allen said, motioning to his right hand. We nodded. We couldn't miss it, it was in the shape of The Lone Star State, and it was about as wide as my forehead, all gold and sparkly.

"Size seventeen," he told us proudly.

"That's big," we all said together.

"Just wait," Jack Allen motioned, and then he reached into his pocket, pulled out a Susan B. Anthony silver dollar and held it up, then took the state of Texas off his finger and held that up, too.

He then passed the silver dollar through opening of the ring, gliding right through without a problem or catch.

Naturally, we gasped.

Jack Allen had done this before, we could tell. I'll bet that he sleeps with that silver dollar, he probably passes that dollar through his ring in his sleep if only to reaffirm his colassalness, but we were mesmerized anyway, even if he was a cab driver with a gimmick. We gave him a big tip.

You know what they say about a man's hands, but we sure as hell weren't going to inquire about that attribute, there was no telling what demonstration lay ahead in that hornet's nest. Jack Allen just might have had a sewer pipe tucked in his back pocket.

I didn't need to see that. A three dollar tip is enough, in my book.

I guess what they say is true.

Everything's bigger in Texas.

Everything's Bigger in Texas, Part Two

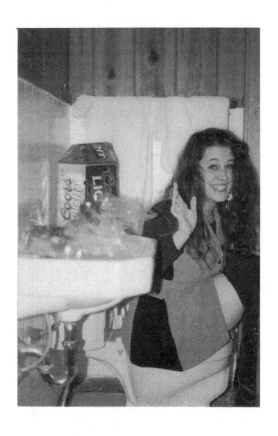

While we were in Austin during our vacation/business trip to South by Southwest, Charlie went for a jog every day. It could have been because on the flight over to Texas, the

woman next to him called him "Fat Boy."
Personally, I think it was because he wanted to
get a little physically fit, since Charlie had told
all of us that sometimes when he was, shall we
say, *in the process of performing intimately with a
lady friend*, he would sometimes painfully cramp
up all over his body.

Anyway, Charlie was always gone for a
good amount of time, and we were never certain
where it was that he was jogging *to*. At first, I
thought he might be jogging around the lake or
by the park that was around our hotel, but I got
a little suspicious when Charlie started coming
back with big bags of food. That's when we had
a group meeting and figured out that he was
running to restaurants or supermarkets. The
"jog" was apparently not a round-trip but a one-
way jog, because it would be pretty hard to
gallop around town with a bucket of fried
chicken in one hand and a tub of coleslaw in the
other.

Food wasn't the only thing that Charlie
brought back with him, because every time
Charlie stepped foot out of our hotel room, he
ran into a celebrity, then would "jog" back to tell
us: "Guess who I saw," Charlie would start as he
began unloading his buffet. "I just saw Dave
Pirner walking down the street, *without Winona
Ryder*."

"Guess who I saw? I just saw Bob Mould
eating lunch."

"Guess who I saw? I just saw Herbert Huncke at the front desk, checking out of the hotel."

"Guess who I saw? I just saw the Ramone who doesn't look like a Ramone."

Well, none of us saw anybody famous unless they were on-stage, but Charlie was bumping into stars left and right, except I did actively recognize Tabitha Soren, but I ignored her because she has a better job than I do.

I wasn't that interested in paying attention to Tabitha Soren, anyway, because I had to go to the bathroom awful bad. I found the toilet by locating the line it had created down the hall, full of 100 skinny blonde girls that urgently needed to use the john to check on potential eye shadow disasters. My bladder was so bloated that it hung over the waistband of my tights like an unwanted appendage or tumor, threatening to rupture with the slightest provocation.

After about twenty minutes, I finally got my turn and I ran in as fast is if someone had told me that Ricki Lake was all doped up on heroin and laying on the bathroom floor with a needle in her chubby little arm. I lifted my bladder, tugged at my tights and sat down, ready to release, ready to free myself, when all of a sudden, the door opened.

This girl walked in, a girl I did not recognize, because after twenty minutes of waiting in line, I was so familiar with the girls behind me that we played "Light As A Feather, Stiff As A Board" for five rounds and cried and hugged one another when it was someone else's turn to pee.

And this was not one of those girls.

"Hi," she said when she walked in.

"Excuse me," I said, because I figured she just got bossy and walked in because the other girls in line had nothing better to do than caucus in front of an unoccupied bathroom.

"Oh, go ahead," she motioned to me as she shut the door.

All of a sudden, I had this really bad feeling, like I was a prisoner in Cell Block H and this girl was about to CLAIM ME FOR HER OWN.

"I won't be long," she added, smiling at me.

"Um, I don't care. I have to piss," I told her.

"And I have to fix my belt," she informed me.

I WAS STUNNED, to say the least, I just couldn't believe it. I was *half naked*. I was *on the toilet*. My *mother* has never even seen me in this position. This girl saw my BUTT. Things like this DO NOT happen. Instead, I decided to say to her after I cleared my throat, *very sternly*, *VERY STERNLY*, (and pointing my finger), "Get Out!", but what came out was

"I AM NOT WIPING IN FRONT OF YOU."

And to that, she kept fixing her belt.

Beat her up, the little voice told me, take that belt, tie her up, pull down her pants and parade her up and down the hall in front of the line, do it, do it, do it! But you can't beat a person up when your tights are around your ankles. When someone's anus is exposed, you can pretty much bet that it's never going to be a fair fight, especially when your dignity levels are already as such a point that the smartest thing to do is stay on the toilet.

I was about to tell her to beat it when she whipped around and left, but not before she held the door open long enough so that all of my other "so-called" friends in line took a peek at me.

I went home. I went back to the hotel, took the rest of the pain pills for my back and turned on the cable.

It was then that I heard God say, "Here, Laurie. This is a little present from me to you because the world is so unfair."

And there on TV, just as if God had sensed my distress and complete humiliation and decided to help me coat my fragmented soul because the pain killers were not going to be enough, was Gregg Allman in *Rush*.

"*Thank you, God,*" I whispered as I cried a little from joy, "*Thank You,*" because God knows how much I love Gregg Allman, and He did the next best thing besides plopping that man right down next to me in person, which would have been better than seeing the girl who saw my butt suddenly lose several teeth and a fat lip when someone fully clothed finally beat her up.

So, for the rest of the night, I sat by myself in the lopsided bed, mesmerized by Gregg Allman on TV, and when it was over, I turned out the light and sang "Tied To The Whipping Post" (the 22-minute version) until I fell blissfully asleep.

The next morning, I woke up because someone was whispering weird little things, and I followed the telephone chord to Charlie's nest, although he was fully covered and underneath the blankets.

"All they've done on this trip is make fun of me," I heard him whisper in secret to the person on the other end, who turned out to be our boss. "I've gone out every night by myself, I've eaten every meal alone, and I'm doing all of my Big Jobs in the hotel lobby bathroom because if I do them in the room, they'll torment me even more."

I started to feel bad, *really bad*, because part of what Charlie was saying was true, even though he left out the parts where he got undressed in front of us, woke us up every morning by ripping up little bits of paper like a rat and annoyed every other passenger on the flight over here by repeatedly insisting that he was "The Worst Lover in the Western Hemisphere."

But still, the three other people in that hotel room, me, Troy and Laura — well, we love Charlie, we have to, he told us where the good places to eat in Austin were. Charlie even brought me a couple of dinners the first nights because my back was so bad that I couldn't walk, although he did lunge on my bed and tickle me, which resulted in further spinal injury so I had to stay in bed for an extra day. But still, we love him, there's no way around it. You just can't help it.

"I'm still having fun," he continued whispering to our boss. "But these are the meanest people I've ever been on vacation with."

I didn't know what to do, there wasn't much of a chance to make it up to Charlie now, we were leaving that day. All I figured that I could do was to be really, really nice to him on the flight home, since I had switched plane tickets with Laura. My original plane ticket was for the following day, as was Troy's, but I was out of money, I was out of energy and I missed my boyfriend, so I cajoled her into trading so I could leave a day earlier.

I was trying super hard to be especially attentive to Charlie, but it was really difficult, because even though the shuttle to the airport was leaving in a half hour, Charlie went back to bed, and I ended up yelling at him. I was still trying when we actually made the already filled shuttle, and in the first three minutes of the ride, Charlie burped so loud in the otherwise morgue-quiet van that the other passengers turned around and looked shamefully at us, and I ended up yelling at him. I decided to keep on trying when we got on the plane and I offered him my trail mix, though all he wanted from me were sex tips. Again, he declared loudly that he was "the Worst Lover in the Western Hemisphere" and wanted to know all of the things that I liked in bed, and after a consistent hour of this, I ended up yelling at him.

After the plane landed and we took Charlie home, he didn't talk to me at all the next day, even when I asked him who was supposed to pick Laura and Troy up from the airport.

Ten minutes later, Troy called the office and said that they had arrived home safely, although at one point, the ride got so bumpy that Laura thought she was going to die and started to shake and sweat. I felt bad about that, since I was supposed to be on that plane, but Troy assured me that after a couple of shots she was fine, and then he told me to sit down, because I was going to be very, very, **very** upset.

I did.

I took a deep breath. "What happened?" I asked.

"Guess who I saw?" Troy said.

"Dave Pirner, Bob Mould, Tabitha Soren and the Ramone that doesn't look like a Ramone," I answered. "We've already played this game."

"Guess who was on the plane with us," Troy goaded me. "Just guess."

"I don't know," I said, a little annoyed. I wanted to tell him about Charlie belching on the shuttle. "Give me a hint."

"He's better than God to you," Troy hinted.

My mind said, "No."

"He was married to Cher," he continued.

"No!"

"He's no angel," he laughed.

"GREGG ALLMAN WAS NOT ON THAT PLANE WITH YOU!" I screamed in denial. "HE WAS NOT!"

"*Was so*," Troy said. "Walked right past Laura on the way to the bathroom, where he stayed for 45 minutes, and then walked right by again. Gave the guy next to us an autographed picture."

All I could do was yell.

Don't Mess With Number 41!

All I wanted was a bagel.

A little piece of round bread with a bit of cream cheese slapped in the middle of it.

It wasn't too much to ask, especially if I was willing to pay for it, and that's exactly what I was thinking as I was waiting in line at Chompie's, the bagel place down the street from my house.

I was really hungry.

I had pulled number 41 from the ticket dispenser, and I held it in my hand, watching the fifteen people ahead of me wave their number frantically as it was called, get served, pay for their stuff and then were on their way. It all looked so easy.

Oh, was I wrong.

When it was finally my turn, and "Number 41" was bellowed over the loudspeaker, I ventured forth and humbly handed the girl behind the counter my number.

She didn't take it.

"How can I help you?" she sighed.

"Bagel and cream cheese," I said plainly, hoping that my simple order wouldn't aggravate her too much.

"You can't get that here," she informed me, despite the fact that I had ordered the same thing for the past ten years at this same counter. "You need to go to the deli counter."

Funny, my mind quirked, I thought I *was* at the deli counter, and then she pointed me in the direction of where they cut the cheese. No pun intended.

There already was an older woman at that counter, and the bagel boy that was helping her was slicing away at a block of cheese. He showed her a piece.

"Not thin enough," she protested. "I need it thin. I need to see through it."

He adjusted his slicer and cut another piece.

He showed it to her.

"Thinner!" she squawked. "How do they teach you to cut cheese here? That's not thin. When I say thin, I mean THIN."

He went back to the slicer. He cut her another piece. This time, I looked at it, too. It was cut so sparsely that it had holes in it.

"You ripped it," the woman said to him, pointing at the holes. "I'm not paying for a quarter pound of ripped cheese."

The bagel boy was getting frustrated, but he complied, and finally came up with a slice of cheese that they both agreed was "thin."

The old woman was happy. The bagel boy was happy. I was happy. I was next.

"And I need a half pound of pastrami, cut semi-thin," the old woman continued. "I need it thick enough so it doesn't fall apart, but thin enough that I don't have to chew on it for an hour."

My blood pressure rose a couple of points.

You already know what happened. It took ten minutes of haggling over the consistency of the friggin' pastrami before she was satisfied with it, and when that situation was resolved, she proceeded to order a pound of corned beef, a half-pound of lox, a quarter-pound of roast beef, a half-pound of Swiss cheese, two loaves of challah (one sliced thin, one sliced thick), a chocolate cake, a quart of matzo ball soup and a big tub of gefilte fish.

All I wanted was a bagel. I had already waited in line — and I am absolutely serious — for forty minutes behind this woman, waiting for my turn. I was hungry, I was getting dizzy, I had developed a bad headache and my whole head was sweating.

Meanwhile, while the old woman was ordering enough food to feed the entire population of Israel plus a kosher suburb of Brooklyn, the son of the deli's owner had hopped behind the counter and had filled the orders of two separate groups of his friends, who, coincidentally, had arrived twenty minutes after I had begun waiting in line.

My blood was pumping through my gray little heart so hard that I thought it was going to start dripping out of my eyes. I was secretly hoping that it would explode in my chest so I could dribble blood and chunky little gray things all over the deli's fine selection of meats and cheeses, in addition to spraying their bagel bins with the spatter of my degenerated internal organs.

I watched as the boy that had been helping the old woman wrapped up her order in five bags, took her money and then gave her the change. I watched him as he got a drink of water, came and stood by the deli counter, not close enough to take my order but close enough to tease me, went and posed at the cash register with his hand on his hip for a minute or two, and — I have to take a deep breath for this part because it torments me simply to remember it — put his mouth up to the microphone and had the complete brashness to call out "**NUMBER 65!**"

My number, still in my hand, now wet and crumpled, the testament to JUST HOW LONG I HAD BEEN plagued by frustration at the bagel place, fell out of my hand and drifted like a leaf towards the filthy floor.

And I flipped out.

"I DON'T BELIEVE THIS!" I screamed, my hands in fists. "This is unreal! AM I INVISIBLE TO YOU PEOPLE? ALL I WANTED WAS A BAGEL!"

And then, because I fully believe that a big vein in my head had burst, filling my skull with bubbly, hot blood, I got even more disoriented and started for the door.

I reached it, ready to push it open, when I stopped.

I whipped around and pointed at the bagel boy, and I know he saw me because *everyone* was staring at me. At that moment, I was a star.

I was ready for my close-up.

"ALL I WANTED WAS A BAGEL!" I said very dramatically. "I DIDN'T EVEN NEED IT SLICED THIN!"

Nobody said anything.

"YOU HAVEN'T HEARD THE LAST OF NUMBER 41 YET!" I continued, shaking. "YOU JUST REMEMBER NUMBER 41!"

And, with that, I headed out to my car. My stomach growled, my head was burning.

I needed revenge, and I got it. I took my $1.50 to Safeway, where I bought a stale bagel in three minutes flat, went home and slapped some butter on it.

They should have known better than to mess with Number 41.

Heat Rations

I don't remember when summer started.

I don't remember the first time this year that I had to keep a potholder in my purse if I needed to open the door of my car.

I don't remember the first time I looked at something in my closet and told myself that it would produce a heat stroke if I wore it.

I don't remember the first time I went to bed wet and naked so I could fall asleep.

I just don't remember.

I am, however, aware of the heat rash in my cleavage, of the sweat that runs over my scalp if I'm outside for more than 14 seconds, and of the fact that unless I sell my car, I'm not going to be able to pay the electric bill in full this month.

I'm sick of summer and I want it to die. I want it to disappear like a bad boyfriend. But it won't. It keeps going on and on, day after day like a steaming yeast infection, except there's no Monistat 7 for five months of three-digit torture. You just have to wait it out and try not to scratch.

There's nothing funny about the summer, plain and simple, especially since, in Phoenix, we only have two seasons—Summer and Before Summer. Air Conditioned and Not Air Conditioned. The Actual Experience or Constant Dreading. Sweating Unpolitely or Just Sweating A Little Bit.

I don't know if this happens to everyone who lives in Phoenix, but I know that it happens to me in every session of Before Summer that I have lived through in this state. I somehow forget what the summer, which is usually immediately before me, feels like.

I can't recall the heat wave that pours out of an cracked car door attached to a vehichle that has been sitting in a parking lot for 30-plus minutes. Or what it feels like to drive that car for the next half hour breathing in nuclear heat that sizzles my lungs until the air conditioner finally kicks in. It escapes me that if I don't wear shoes, the simmering sidewalk will eat through the flesh of my feet to my ankles. I don't recall that I have to change my underwear four times a day or experience Jungle Rot in my crotch. And that means putting on a clean pair, not just turning the ones you're wearing inside out and putting them back on again.

I somehow lose my memory of the unbearable during those quieter Before Summer months, it quickly fades out of my consciousness for my own protection, I'm sure. Every once in a while, however, I'll experience a flashback, say like when I'm cooking a turkey and need to baste it. I'll open the oven door, my glasses will fog up, the heat flashes me like in menopause and a little voice in my head sings "That felt like Summer." It's a bad, smelly feeling.

Last year, on one of those 120-something days, I had had it. Something snapped, broke loose and floated around in my bubbling brain until I decided that I needed to blame somebody for the heat. I became convinced that it had to be somebody else's fault that enough steam was rising off my body to smoothe out the dirty hamper wrinkles in my clothes. I called my mother. She answered.

I cleared my throat.

"I demand to know why you decided in 1972 that we needed to live in a desert."

"Is this part of your therapy?" she asked.

"No," I insisted. "I'm just very hot and it's your fault."

"Are you high on drugs?" she replied.

"If only," I stressed. "I want to know why we moved from New York to Arizona."

"Oh," she said suddenly. "Because the roaches were enormous in Florida and we had too many relatives that already lived there."

Ewww. Florida. I had no idea. *I almost moved to Florida?* I'd rather live in New Jersey than Florida. Hell, I'd rather live *here* than in Florida. Some people would argue that at least in Florida, there's an ocean. They don't have much to say after you remind them that they will be steamed to death like a dumpling before they get there.

So, being that I had no scapegoat since my parents actually had saved me *somewhat*, I decided to do the next best thing. I was going to ignore the summer.

And I did. I had no job to speak of, I had no daytime obligations. I closed the blinds to my bedroom window, tacked a black sheet over it and went to bed.

I didn't get out of bed until the sun had done more than slipped out of the sky, it had to be dead and buried in China before I left the house. Most of my friends had adapted the same schedule, since a hefty portion of them didn't have jobs, either. We became summer vampires, coming out only after dark and scurrying for shelter once the sun threatened to rise.

We had become nocturnal, like every other species of being that has survived in the desert for thousands of years.

It was the best summer I've ever had in this city. I didn't mind the heat at all, mainly because I wasn't actively involved in it. I had made a conscious decision to live an alternative climate crafted lifestyle. And I'd do it again, except that now I do have a job that forces me to remain awake for some of the daylight hours.

And daylight is a constant reminder that there isn't enough shaded parking in Phoenix, that the only time my window shield pops opens without a struggle is when I'm driving and that the heat somehow makes people believe that summertime is a free-for-all fashion show. It makes them think that the heat is a non-conditional entitlement to wear clothes they have no business walking around public places in. Let us all remember that spandex is a priveledge, not a right. It should be treated accordingly and with a certain amount of respect. One more walnut-shaped nub in the central region of a gentleman's shiny bike shorts is a sight that these eyes can no longer bear. Nor is a stretched-out swinging breast that peeks out every now and then from a precarious tank top. The summer is obscene.

What eats at me the most is that it's October and it's still summer here. Yes, it is. This weather in any other part of the country is considered SUMMER. If my butt is still sweating, it's still HOT. No one's butt should ever sweat. It's a violation of your civil rights, you should be able to live peacefully in any habitat without butt condensation. What's even worse is that the amount that's on either cheek is nothing compared to what's dripping from underneath my bra.

And right now I want to be cold. I want my teeth to shiver. I want to see the steam rising from my coffee and shooting from my nostrils. I want to use my comforter, I wanna wear a pair of socks and a sweater. I want my nose to run without the aid of a bronchial or sinus infection.

I WANT TO TAKE A HOT SHOWER, FOR CHRIST'S SAKE!

Take a deep breath, I have to tell myself, a deep, hot breath. Relax. (I *did* learn this in therapy.) When Christmas arrives in a little shy of three months, when you're drinking steaming coffee and licking snot off of your upper lip, when a hot shower isn't enough to make you feel warm and there's two comforters on your bed, you won't remember any of this. Not one thing, not even moist ass print you leave every time you stand up.

It will all be gone.

Now count to three and open your eyes and realize that although it may be bad here, although it may be hot, you *don't* live in Miami.

Flea Bag

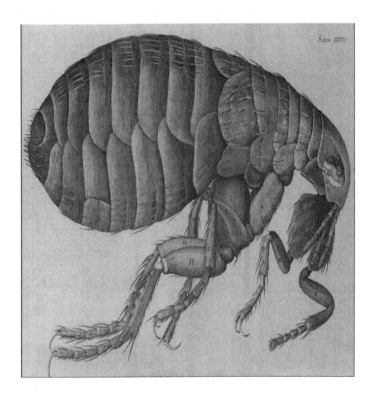

Something bit me.

I knew this because my stomach itched, and when I scratched it, I saw a small little red mark. It looked like a spider bite, and I kept messing with it until it bled, mostly because I always considered scabs the best form of self-contained, free entertainment.

After the day that my belly got bit, my leg itched, and when I looked at it, I had another small little red mark on my calf. More fun, I thought, so I scratched that one, too.

Several days after that, there wasn't a place on my big-girl body that didn't have at least one red mark on it, and it kinda scared me. Everything itched, and sometimes, I could even feel the little sting of the bite, but when I went to search for the culprit, there was nothing there. The fun of the scabs had worn off, especially after I had about fifty of them, and I started wearing pantyhose to bed.

It was then that we noticed the cat.

He was itchy, too.

In fact, he couldn't stop scratching himself.

My cat, Barnaby, was a flea bag.

And so was I.

In that moment, I started feeling them crawling everywhere, on my head, in my ears, under my arms and in my naughty bits. I took a shower. I took two. I just knew that those fleas had laid eggs everywhere on me, in my clothes, in my bed, in my hair. My mind flashed back to third grade when the nurse used to check us for head lice, and I never had it, but at least there was a shampoo for that. If I had fleas, I was going to have to make an appointment at the Humane Society to get myself dipped.

What the hell was I going to do? I could just imagine those damn fleas jumping off my head, biting people that I worked with, and soon everybody would start calling me "Bugger" or "Larvae Laurie." People would begin to shy away from me, saying, "My mom said you can't come to our house because you're a dirty girl," and then soon, a practical joker would lay a Hartz "2 in 1" collar on my desk at the office. I was going to be the biggest joke around the place since we found out that Charlie, our ad guy, had been peeing in an Evian bottle because it was too much effort to get up and walk to the bathroom.

So I called the vet and to my relief found out fleas pretty much don't like people anyway, but also that soap and plain old shampoo kills them, and since I had been washing on a pretty regular basis, I was relieved.

But I still had a problem. The fleas liked Barnaby, and as long as he was a willing host, we were still going to have our little guests bed and breakfasting in my room and on my body.

There was only one thing I could do, and that was mass annhiliation. Bring out the big guns. I was going to bomb. That is, if I survived giving my cat a flea bath.

So I ventured to PetSmart, where the responsible pet owners shop, like my sister and her husband, spending thousands of dollars on rawhide bones, leather leashes and fancy pants dog food. My sister's dog, Maggie, is a maniac Rottweiler who sleeps on a nicer bed than I do. It has flannel sheets. Maggie also gets groomed on a regular basis, not because she needs it, but to "improve her socialization skills." The cat box at my house, on the other hand, only gets cleaned out when the dogs wander in and help themselves to the snack tray.

Anyway, there I was at PetSmart, standing in line like the neglegent pet owner I was, my arms full of cheapest "Flee-B-Gone" products I could find. The cashier rang up the goods and looked at me in disgust. "That will be $47.88," he said, shaking his head, which was thinking, "Bad Cat Lady. BAD. I'm gonna report you. I bet you have two hundred cats at your house, most of which are DEAD, Dr. Mengele!"

He threw my stuff in a defective bag that only had one handle, and I started to leave. As I looked up, however, I was staring right into a very familliar face, which was loaded with astonishment. It was my sister's boss.

"Why Laurie," she said, "What are you doing here?"

"Getting some stuff for my cat," I said quickly, since I already knew that she was an even more devoted pet owner than my sister was. Her dogs get their portraits done by Olan Mills. I know because I've seen them.

"I just got some treats for the dogs," sister's boss said, pulling out a box from her bag that looked like the Milano mint cookies from Pepperidge Farm.

"That's nice," I smiled. "Well, gotta go!"

"What did you get?" she said, peering in my bag, which was gaping open because I could only hold one side of it.

"Oh," she said quietly when she saw the flea bath, the flea bomb, the flea comb and the flea collar.

I could tell right there and then that she was going to report me, too. "Well, no wonder," she was thinking. "Her sister told me her house looked like 'Sanford and Son,' ONLY DIRTIER."

That night, my boyfriend and I hunted Barnaby down. We had already discussed the strategy of the Flea Blood Bath, considering the scars on my arms that were sustained from the last time I tried to get him near water, but that to everyone else looks like a serious suicide attempt.

We contemplated drugging him, but we didn't feel like sharing, so we devised a plan we had seen on TV in rodeos. Corbett had the rope, I was going to hold him down, and we were going to string Barnaby up like a pig and then dip him into the bath upside down. It seemed logical and the best possible plan.

We were ready. I was going to head the cat off at the pass and corner him, Corbett had the lasso whipping around in the air. We moved in.

Instead, Barnaby rolled over and looked at us like the idiots we are, and just sat there. We couldn't believe it. He was going to go peacefully, he had basically offered himself to us. Here I am, wash me, you fools. We weren't going to need the kitty straightjacket after all.

Barnaby was so cooperative he basically gave himself the bath, and the only casualty that occured was when I accidentally splashed myself in the eyes with the poison. It was a miracle, although it really hurt, and has made my vision very blurry.

The next morning, after I took all of the pets to my sister's, I began bombing the house, and I read the directions super carefully with my good eye. I pulled the tab to release the fogger, which shot directly into my face, because my good eye isn't as smart as my bad eye and got the words "pull" and "push" confused. It wasn't as bad as the time I maced myself, but I would say it was pretty equal to the time when I tried to wash the kitchen floor with straight bleach.

The house started filling up with chemicals, and I left for work, with the hiss of the foggers sounding like a thousand snakes. It was scary.

It wasn't as scary, though, as the thought of sharing my bed with eight thousand fleas. I'd rather remember Itchy and Scratchy as pieces of harmless annimation instead of squatters in my pubic hair.

Please Be a Chocolate Chip

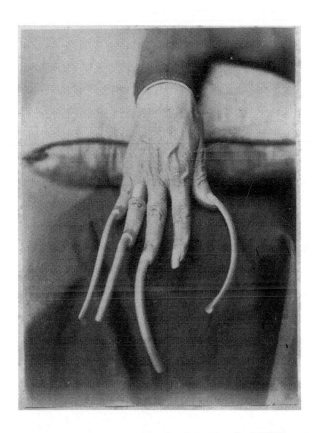

I scooped chocolate rasperry gelato into my mouth with glee, straight from the carton.
With the last spoonfull aimed at my tongue, I shoveled the ice cream into my mouth and swished the last bit around, savoring it when I noticed something weird.

There was a little, pointy hard thing in my mouth.

It was not ice cream.

Oh, no, I prayed, please don't let it be something gross.

I told myself not to look at it as I picked it out of my mouth.

It's probably just a chocolate chip, I tried to tell myself. A concavem bony sharp chocolate chip that nicked my tongue like a razor.

I've had experience with this sort of situation before; it happened at a hamburger place not far from the ASU campus. I had taken to eating there on a very regular basis, as in three times a week or so. My skin broke out, but my belly loved it, that is until one day I bit into my cheeseburger, and as I was chewing, I felt a little, pointy hard thing in my mouth.

Immediately, I was befuddled and spit it out into a napkin, expecting a nasty piece of fat or a bone. I could not have, in any humanly way possible, been prepared for what I saw staring back at me admist chewed meat on that white napkin.

It was a fingernail.

But it wasn't **just** a fingernail. It was a pinky nail, a long pinky nail, easily measurable to a quarter of an inch long.

With hot pink fingernail polish on it.

Oh, my stomach tried like hell to jump up to my mouth, but I held it down, composed myself and took the body part to the guy at the register. I had two choices; I could vomit or I could exact justice.

"I found this in my hamburger," I said as I presented it to him.

"Ewww," he said, recoiling with disgust.

"It doesn't belong to me," I said, holding out my hands. "It's not my color."

He nodded. "We grind our own meat," he assured me, as if that made everything okay.

"Well, you can have this," I assured him as I handed back my meal.

"Did you want another one?" he asked me politely.

"Do I look like a spider to you?" I responded politely. "I've had enough of eating my own kind for today."

"Would you like a chicken sandwich instead?" he offered.

"No," I declined as I sighed. "It might turn out to be someone's big toe."

Needless to say, I never ate there again, in fact, I quit eating any kind of ground meat, human or otherwise, unless I was at my Nana's or my own house.

So I was already familiar with the texture and taste of a stranger's fingernail by the time I had eaten the pint of gelato in despair.

I couldn't look at what I pulled out of my mouth this time, so I closed my eyes and handed it to my boyfriend.

"Ewww," he said as he studied it. "That's pretty gross."

"It's what I thought it was, huh?" I said, my eyes still shut.

"Yep," he answered.

"Does it have fingernail polish on it?"

"Uh, no. This one belongs—*belonged*—to a guy."

This time I screamed, and I screamed until my throat hurt. I screamed because I know what guys do with their hands. I know where they put them. I was willing to bet that that fingernail had been down more pairs of pants than just his own. And I knew, that in his own, he had *scratched*.

Tile

Sometimes I get in these moods.

They're frantic, desperate moods, and I know that when they hit, they need to be addressed right away.

The last fit I had hit me and consumed me in a matter of seconds, I didn't plan it.

It was TILE.

I just walked out of my front door one day, onto my porch and I felt it sock me in the gut.

TILE.

I've been hit by tile before. I happened six years ago, one early day in May, and before I knew it, I had a truck load of dried, red Mexican clay sitting in my driveway. I, on the other hand, was on my hands and knees in my family room spreading 200 pounds of mixed concrete, 85 pounds of which remained in my hair for five months.

TILE.

I've also been hit by wood, since another day I woke up and I felt the need to **build** something. I didn't know what I should build, a shelf, a napkin holder, an ark? I went to Home Depot, bought an electric saw and screwdriver and before the sun set, I had two new bookcases. The next week, I built an entertainment center.

For my birthday that year, I got an electric sander. For Christmas, I got a radial arm saw.

Before I knew it, my inner carpenter had created a wood floor in my living room.

Then, I learned how to drink whiskey straight out of the bottle, and I didn't build silly things anymore, that period of my life was over, especially since the period in my life in which I saw daylight was over.

A robber came over one day and stole my tools, and I didn't care, I didn't need them anymore, they were all rusty anyway. The saws were gone, my sander with them, as were my routers, screwdrivers and drills. My washer and dryer were also thieved. It turned out that I really wasn't burglarized, but broken up with, since my ex-boyfriend had moved out and had taken his gifts with him, though it took me a couple of days to realize it.

I didn't argue with him to get any of the stuff back, because I simply had more important things to do, like go out. It didn't matter anymore.

So several weeks ago when I felt the tile fever in my blood, I was naturally surprised. I thought the busy bee in me was dead.

It wasn't. It was just taking a nap.

I took a deep breath. The drinking days have been over by about a year, I guessed that it was a good time to start a new hobby.

The porch *needed* to be tiled.

It needed to be tiled *soon.*

I was convinced that I could not bear another day of living with an un-tiled porch.

So my boyfriend, who knows absolutely nothing about tools, and I returned to my old stomping grounds, Home Depot, to fetch my needed supplies.

I was standing in the tile aisle, trying to decide which type we liked best.

A friendly-looking gent in an orange apron wandered over and asked if we needed help.

"As a matter of fact, we do," I said. "I need 150 square feet of Super Tile."

The guy looked through me and straight to my boyfriend for confirmation.

"One hundred and fifty square feet of this?" he said, patting a carton of Super Tile.

"Yes," I reiterated, as he started to load it into our cart.

"You got it, sir," he said with a big smile to my boyfriend. "And you'll also need about 50 pounds each of concrete and grout."

"Um," my boyfriend said. "I'm not—"

"And you'll need sealer, too, because this tile is porous."

"I know," I said, getting a little mad.

He motioned to my boyfriend. "I'd recommend this sealer right here, give it two coats."

"Don't tell me," he answered. "Tell *her*. She's the one who's doing it."

The orange apron jester man took two steps backwards as if my boyfriend had wiggled his tongue at him. Written all over his face was horror and disgust, as if his manly mind was spitting out, over and over again in Testosterone Morse Code, "Dude. GOD MADE YOU BIGGER THAN HER FOR A REASON."

The jester cleared his throat, laughed to himself, and then began to describe in detail, step by step, how tile is laid, beginning with how to take the tiles out of the box.

Could you blame him? I'm only a woman, after all.

Women can't lay tile. Women can't put down wood floors. Women can't build bookcases or entertainment centers. One of their nails may break, or they might have a super bad period and bleed all over everything.

"I've done this before," I said sternly.

He laughed at me again, this time to my face.

"But I'm telling you how to do it **right**," he emphasized.

My boyfriend took the cart and wheeled it away, far enough down the aisle so he wouldn't be hit with pointy shards of flying tile. He knew that I was going to kill this man, this man who had already decided that I couldn't do it because I was a girl, this man who thought that the only things that women should lay were horny, stupid, desperate men, this man who had never laid tile in his life because everything he told me so far had been **wrong.**

All of these things were flying through my head in a furious red blur, and I raised my shaking, infuriated hand to point at him.

You have no business working in this store.

I have done more things than you're even capable of.

You're the reason most women don't wander out of the gardening department.

Are you in some sort of a men's drum circle club?

Asshole.

But I didn't say anything. What I knew I could do was more important than what he didn't think I could do.

The next thing I knew, I was on my hands and knees, spreading mixed concrete, most of which was not only in my hair but in my eyes.

I spread the concrete.

I laid the tile.

I grouted it.

I sealed it.

I took a picture of it, and as soon as it gets developed, I'm going back to Home Depot to find the jester, because I'm good at laying tile.

I taught my boyfriend how do it.

Poor thing.

For his birthday this year, he's getting a tool belt and a table saw, since I decided just this morning that our lives would be so much happier if the bedroom had a wood floor.

Too Late

It was a Friday when my Pop Pop called me and I heard the news.

As I returned the phone to its cradle, I immediately reached for my car keys in a desperate and selfish effort to save myself. It was the survival instinct kicking in, taking charge, telling me that I had to get to the nearest store and get there quickly, there was no time to waste.

Marlboros, it had just been reported, had been poisoned and were being recalled.

I had to get there before all of the Marlboros were taken off the shelves, poisoned or not. My heart was pounding, my flesh was sweating, *where were my keys?* I ransacked my bed for the sound of them, scoured the bathroom and was about to dive into the kitchen when I heard the panicked, stampeding feet of horses. I looked up and saw, through my bedroom window, The Four Riders of The Apocalypse galloping down my street, headed for the corner Circle K.

It was then that I knew it was true, the unspeakable had happened.

I was too late.

Oh God, I was too late!

I heard the whine of the sirens in the distance, the sky turned black with boiling red clouds.

The only thing I could do was find every last cigarette, butt and flake of tobacco and hoard them.

To say that I wasn't very lucky would be putting it quite mildly. As it happened, I had gotten paid that day but didn't have enough time to go to Costco to get my standard two cartons. Instead, I had the remnants of the last two cartons from the payday two weeks before, which screeched in with a grand total of seven whole cigarettes, three half-smoked cigarettes and five butts with at least three drags left on each.

I packed them all in a double-bagged Ziploc baggie and submerged them in the water tank behind the toilet.

Drastic measures, you say, perhaps silly, extreme, desperate? Well, all I knew is that of the tens of thousands of people that I know who smoke, fifty percent of those smoke Marlboros, and I knew that once they were down to their lucky cigarette, it would be my door they'd be breaking through with a pick ax trying to get their fix.

Addicts are not very pretty people.

And I, as an addict, was going to protect my stash.

I got a pen and paper and figured out a ration schedule to see how long my smokes would hold out until the relief packages of Marlboros arrived.

I wasn't going to last more than two hours.

I felt my heart drop.

So I decided that I would only be able to smoke under the most necessary and dire of conditions, which was doing my morning business. And, as I know, it takes three cigarettes to complete the entire transaction until the final flush, so I was safe for three days, but I figured if I ate an abundance of raw vegetables, especially broccoli, I might be able to last longer.

If this sounds odd to any of you non-smokers, let me recall the story of my friend Doug who had trouble one day, let's just say doing his duty on the throne. He mentioned this enigma to another friend of his, who promptly and respectfully solved the problem by sticking a cigarette in Doug's mouth, lit it and then sent him back to the potty, adding quietly, "You know not what you do." From that day forward, no one I know ever saw Doug go into a bathroom, public or private, without a smoke in one hand and a dirty magazine in the other. It was a done deal.

The obvious solution to The Great Marlboro Embargo of 1995 would be, quite naturally, to switch brands until the cyanide or insecticide was removed from the filters of the contaminated cigarettes, but this I could not bring myself to do.

Last year, during my birthday season, only one birthday card sailed through the post office and to my house. I didn't recognize the return address; it was from Sioux Falls, South Dakota. I pondered, I studied the envelope. Then I opened it. On the front of the card was a valley drenched with autumn, a small farmhouse, a trail of wild horses, and the snow on top of blue, peaked mountains. Inside, the card read in big, crimson letters, "In a land this big, you can't dream small. Happy Birthday from Marlboro Country." Tucked in the seam of the card was a present for me, 100 bonus Country Store Miles to go toward the Marlboro casket or oxygen tent of *my choice*. I was stunned. I was moved. I was crying.

I made a commitment, you see, when I was fourteen and took my first drag off of a Marlboro Red while hiding in a desert lot across the street from my high school. My head whipped off my shoulders, spinning in the sky until I had plant my denim Sassooned butt in the dirt, but I knew I had found something that I couldn't live without.

Fifteen years later, the desert lot is gone, built up into condos which I accidentally set a little on fire during the construction stage the following year, but the commitment is still there. It has to be there. Black stuff starts bubbling like Texas tea out of my chest when I try to take the commitment away. I know for a fact that my lungs contain enough tar to pave every cross-country highway in the continental United States.

My boyfriend came home later that night and asked me if I had heard the news, and I nodded.

"Were you able to buy any cigarettes today?" he asked.

"No," I said, as I shook my head sadly.

"Me either," he added. "And I don't have any left."

Oh no. Oh boy. Oh shit. Seven cigarettes. Divided by two. Equaled *not enough for me to share*.

"Me, too," I sinned.

"It's going to be a rough couple of days," he sighed.

I agreed. Life during wartime.

So I made dinner, we rented a movie in which the characters chain-smoked. I hate that. Three hours had passed since I had had my last puff. I started to shake a little, and then I got dizzy. I began to cough. I had to do *something*.

"I'll be right back," I said, getting up. "I have to go to the bathroom."

He didn't suspect a thing.

I ran to the bathroom, pulled the lid off the tank and the bag out of the water. I carefully chose one of the half-smoked ones, since this situation didn't classify as a biological emergency.

I took the first hit. Instantly, my hands became steady, my lungs stopped percolating. My head cleared.

I was alive again.

Each subsequent drag tasted as good as the first, and I sucked on that thing until the filter began to glow.

I walked back into the living room and sat down next to my boyfriend, who was fully engrossed in the movie, watching people smoke and smoke and smoke.

"Isn't it funny," he said after a couple of minutes, "That I want a cigarette so bad after watching these people smoke, that actually I *smell* it."

"It's amazing what the mind can do," I agreed.

"You don't smell that?" he asked.

"Nope," I said, shaking my head.

He looked at me.

"Do that again," he requested.

"Do what?" I questioned.

"Shake your head."

"Why?" I said, my face getting pretty hot.

"That smell is coming from you, it's coming from your head," he said suspiciously. "Shake your head, honey."

"NO."

"SHAKE YOUR HEAD, HONEY."

"NO!"

"You have smoke hair! It's on you, I can smell it!" he cried. "Where are they? The bathroom? *Of course* they're in the bathroom!"

"It's just my regular smell," I protested. "It's my scent!"

"You're hoarding, you foul temptress! ADDICT! You have to share! It's in the rules!"

"I MADE A COMMITMENT!" I yelled. "THEY SENT ME A BIRTHDAY CARD!"

"And I bought you a carton for your birthday!" he replied.

I broke down, he was right. It's in the rules, despite survival of the fittest or most addicted.

"But what about my morning business?" I whimpered as he led me down the hall towards the bathroom.

"We'll just eat lots of broccoli and Mexican food," he said, but not after I lifted up the lid of the water tank and handed him the dripping bag.

That Bitch From the Paper

Something rather weird has happened.

People, I am told, hate me.

HATE me.

Especially girls, in fact, mostly girls.

I'm not sure if I understand this. While I think it's within somebody's rights to hate anyone they feel like hating, like Shannen Dougherty or Courtney Love or ME, it's still a weird thing.

I've had people become very angry with me, like my mother because I went shopping on her credit card, or an ex-boyfriend because I set all of the love notes from his previous girlfriend on fire, or the attorney general's office for writing bad checks, but hate is a far different word. HATE is a strong word, conceived from the immaculate love of Loathing and Spite.

My friend Russ was the first person to tell me that people Hated Me, predominantly his girlfriend, and I was a little taken aback. Not because I am such a giving, loving, warm person that I'm up for canonization, but because the people that hated me didn't know me. They had never even met me. I had never stolen their boyfriends, I had never made fun of what they were wearing, and I had never singed their hair on purpose with a lit cigarette.

When Russ initially told me of this venom epidemic, I became slightly obsessed with it. I wanted to know why, what I had done or said to create this. Russ just shook his head.

"She just hates you, that's all," he said. "I'm not even allowed to talk to you."

Just then another friend of mine sat at the table, and when I told him about it, he laughed.

"Yeah," he said, "My girlfriend hates you, too."

"Why?" I asked.

"I don't know. All I know is that there's a bunch of people that hate you. They call you 'that bitch from the paper.'"

"Oh," I said, trying to absorb it.

Then he pointed out people at the bar.

"*His* girlfriend hates you, *his* girlfriend also hates you, and so does *his*," he explained.

"But I don't know their girlfriends," I insisted, thinking that I should have done something to deserve this fine award, like if any of them had ever bought me a drink or that I was considered even remotely pretty, but their hate, sadly, was unfounded.

It's not that I haven't ever done anything bad that exempts me from having certain people dislike me a lot. That's not true. I know that there are a handful of individuals that cannot stand the sight of me, but at least I know why. My friend Dave's girlfriend despises me because I stuck a barbequed beef rib in her mailbox that made her and Dave break up. I can accept her hate. There's my mailman that leaves me nasty notes in my mailbox that says I need to pick up my mail more than just one time a month, and who withholds my mail until I do. It's fine for him to hate me.

I deserve hate in those proportions.

But not from people that I haven't gotten my fun from, that part isn't fair. Maybe I should make them hate me more. Maybe they hate me because their boyfriends like hanging around me better. Maybe they hate me because I'm smarter. Maybe they hate me because I wear nicer clothes. Maybe they hate because I don't have to work because I'm an heiress. Maybe they hate me because I'm beautiful. And, hopefully now, they'll hate me more.

Maybe they hate me because I'm about to call them a bunch of Cackling Hens, the kind of girls that don't have anything better to do than sit around and drink flavored coffee in between yeast infections and talk about how bored they are, so they need a hobby. And Hate is a great hobby. It can use up all of your spare time before you know it. You get to dissect all of somebody else's flaws and personality disorders, all the while making yourself supreme, more worthy, superior to someone else.

Maybe I should stumble around town and pick out people that I hate because I don't like the color of lipstick that they're wearing, or because they once made my boyfriend laugh, or because I didn't like something they said. Maybe then I could make myself feel better, raise my own low-self esteem, eliminate my depression and give my psychiatrist her walking papers. "I don't need you anymore," I could tell my doctor. "I've found someone to hate." It sounds a whole lot better than going on a diet.

And I have hated people before. I hated a girl in fifth grade because she could do a better backbend than me. I hated the girl who went to prom with the boy that I wanted to go with. I hated the girl that my boyfriend got pregnant and then married. I hated the boys in the parking lot at Balboa Cafe that called me

"Hagatha" as they climbed into a Lexus. I hated Courtney Love because she was obnoxious and stupid and needed to do her roots.

And then one day I realized that I didn't hate Courtney Love at all. It was way worse than that, way worse than hate.

It was jealousy.

I was jealous because she was doing what I wanted to do, she was being who I wanted to be, she had the great band, she had the prettier dresses, she had better hair, now she has perkier breasts, and she did it all before I did. I hated myself for not hating her.

Then I found out I had a crush on her.

I am in love with Courtney Love.

Now my boyfriend hates her.

All I'm saying is have at least one good point, something stable and solid that you can list as a reason. All I'm saying is be fair; give me a chance, let me make you hate me. Hate me because I'm rude, or a drunk, or because I don't shave. Don't just detest me for nothing at all. We could even have a backbend contest to seal it.

After all, hate is a terrible thing to waste.

Drop Dead Ted

If you've heard it already, I'll confirm the rumor. It's true: I have a soft spot in my heart for Ted Kaczynski.

No, it's not one of the spots that has turned black, rotten and soggy because of bitterness and rage (those spots are reserved for ex-boyfriends, ex-bosses and close family members), but a genuine little spot that belongs directly to Ted, and not just because we have the same hair (mine happened post-perm). A couple of days ago, that little spot wept when I heard that Ted was found half-naked (the naughty bits half) in his jail cell after trying to hang himself with his own little panties.

Let me say right now that I'm not the kind of girl that's attracted to convicts already in prison—I've only dated men on parole or probation. I would never be a "pen" pal of a prisoner (although my mother insisted that I write to a soldier during that Desert Storm thing because I might get a husband out of it. As soon as I told my soldier boy that I wasn't "a pixie of a woman" he never wrote back. Friendly fire? I think not). I've only had one other brush with a renown criminal figure, and that was when I was five and lived in Brooklyn and went to a friend's house to play and show off my new Partridge Family book cover, which came free inside of the "School Days" album. Inadvertently, I forgot the book on a bench in front of their house, and when I went back to get it, I saw their mean old grandfather tearing Keith Partridge's loving smile in half. I started to cry, and my mother hit me. "Don't you ever say a word!" she hissed at me. I never understood why until 20 years later when I asked her about it, and she nearly spit out her coffee. "Jesus, Mary and Joseph, that wasn't some crazy old man, Laurie," she informed me. "That was Carlos Gambino!" But—and I've been dying to say this—I digress.

My relationship with Ted started on my honeymoon. My groom and I were driving from

Chico Hot Springs, Montana, to Helena, and as soon as we hit the highway, we heard the news: The Unabomber had been caught! In Montana! And, he was, at that very same moment, being transported to the county courthouse in the state's capitol, Helena.

It didn't take long to figure out that something really huge was up as we rolled into town. Big things were happening. People were jittery, anxious and cautious. The courthouse, which was one block from our inn, was swarmed with news people, cameramen, satellite dishes and big trucks. The Unabomber wasn't the only local celebrity in the jail, either: the Big Cheese Freeman leader was also being arraigned.

People were going NUTS. No one could talk about anything else. We pulled into a Conoco to get gas and the attendant asked us, without blinking, if we were in Helena because of the Unabomber.

When we arrived at our bed & breakfast inn, the innkeeper opened the door and said immediately, "Did you hear about the Unabomber? I feel so sorry for him. All he had was a bike and he had to make his own screws! The poor little Unabomber!"

"Boy," I said, shaking my head. "Think of what he could have done with public transportation and a Home Depot!"

I feel sorry for the Unabomber, though, only because the Montana press (who repeatedly kept spelling his title as "Unabomer" on the front page) was running a fine tooth comb through his life, and absolutely nothing of any great interest was popping up. A front page story the next morning recounted the chilling tales of the Unabomber's semi-frequent trips to Helena in which he would stay in really cheap motels, buy only bottled water from the convenience store next to it and sometimes patronized a used bookstore, but never spent more than a dollar. They also mentioned that they suspected that his bombs arrived without postmarks because the only friend Ted had was the postman, and when the postman wanted a day off, Ted would just hop on his bike and take over for him. And mail his bombs.

Even as we journeyed to Glacier National Park the next day, people kept asking us if we had come to Montana for the Unabomber, almost as if he was equivalent to the Pope. I kept wanting to say, "Oh, no, no, no. We were here for the Freeman, way before this trendy Unabomber thing sprang up," but my husband was afraid it would be enough to get us shot.

People are like that in Montana, but I ask you one thing: If Ted Kaczynski had my Partridge Family book cover in his hands, would he tear it up?

I think not — but I digress.

Poor little Unabomber.

"Do You Have Laurie's Car?"

There I was There I was There I was,
where else, sitting on a bar stool at Long
Wong's on Friday night, sippin' whiskey,
smoking cigarettes and laughing. It had turned
out to be a fairly prosperous evening, which
meant that although I was broke, I was drinking.
Jerry was buying since he had just gotten paid,
Nikki and I were gulping, the night was still

somewhat young and we were having fun by inserting tampons into other people's beer bottles when they weren't looking.

That's when I spotted my friend Patti.

He didn't look so good. In fact, he looked horrible. His skin had become transparent and glossy, his beer mug dangled from his fingers at a dangerously low angle, and he was staring at the ground.

"Are you all right?" I yelled from my seat.

He shook his head. "I'm gonna take a cab home," he answered. "I feel a little sick. Alcohol poisoning again."

"You'll have to wait for forty-five minutes for a cab," I told him. "You don't look like you have that long. I'll take you home."

He nodded, and I grabbed my purse, took his hand and headed out the door.

Hand in hand, we played the real-life version of Frogger, dashing in between traffic as we crossed the street to where my car was. I was hurrying, because by my estimation of how long Patti had been parked on that bar stool, he only had a good 15 minutes of consciousness left, at best. I was losing him fast, his hand had grown limp and I was basically dragging him, he stumbled along behind me with his eyes closed and his hair in his face.

Oh no, I thought, I've seen this look before. I've seen it on my friend Doug's face one night as we were driving out of the same parking lot that I was now standing in. Doug was stretched out in the passenger seat, his head tipped back and his eyes resting, when all of a sudden he lurched forward, screamed, "How do you work these goddamn space age windows?" turned and then produced the biggest curtain of vomit I had ever seen in my life, draped over the closed glass, the dashboard, car door and the front of his shirt. It was quite a production, and most of it is still there to this day. He wiped his mouth with his soaked shirt, asked for a shot out of my bottle, which I gave him, and the color returned to his placid face. He informed me that he now felt "reborn," although I made him ride with his head far out the window, like a dog, until we got to the next bar.

I was not taking that chance with Patti, and was going to make sure that I rolled down the window first thing when we got into the car, and I told Patti that. I kept telling him that as we wandered up and down the line of cars in front of 6 East, where I was sure I had parked it.

"Patti, I parked the car right here," I stressed. "Right here, were this red Bronco is now parked."

"Are you sure?" he questioned. "Sometimes your memory isn't so good."

"I know what happened to my car," I announced, ignoring him. "It's been *stolen!*"

"Your memory *is* shit, Laurie," Patti said, laughing at me. "If you think your car's been stolen, you don't remember what it looks like on the inside, besides the smell of it. No thief in their right mind would steal that car. You have to sit with your knees up to your ears because the level of the trash on the floor is equal to the seat. What happened the last time you went to get your oil changed?"

"The man wanted to dump out the ashtray," I mentioned.

"And . . . . .?"

"And when he tried to vacuum it out, the hose got clogged."

"Why?"

I sighed. I hated this. "Because all of the butts and the gum kind of molded together into, well, kind of a sculpture."

"What happened to the man's vacuum hose?"

Silence.

"What happened to the hose, Laurie?"

I whispered the answer.

"What happened?"

"It exploded, okay? The hose exploded and my ashtray broke the man's vacuum cleaner. That doesn't change the fact that my car has been stolen."

"Your car hasn't been stolen," Patti shouted, exasperated. "It has not been stolen! *It's been towed!*"

I gasped. And then I got scared, because all of a sudden, it became my fault. If my car had been stolen, I was a victim who could possibly get a new car, maybe something convertible and sporty. If my car had been towed, as Patti suspected, I was nothing but a Gilligan, I was going to have to find it then pay to get a car back that no one would ever want to steal in the first place.

So I marched up to 6 East, and confronted the bouncer, who, when he stepped away from the door, revealed a handwritten sign that proclaimed, "If you park out in front, you must come in here first or your car will be towed," which amazed me, because every single word on the sign was spelled *right*.

Patti was right. My car had been towed.

The next thing I did was go back to Long Wong's to tell Nikki and Jerry, mostly to get sympathy. I was telling them the story, my hands waving in the air to make it even better, stomping my foot every now and then for emphasis. *Those assholes! Can you believe it? They towed my car! I don't have any money, I'm broke! What the hell am I going to do? What if I had left a sleeping child in the backseat? Son of a bitch! They're messing with the wrong car! Now I have to give them seventy-five bucks to get my car back! I don't have that kind of money!*

Jerry, whose eyes had already swung into half-mast by this time, fumbled for his wallet, dropped it a couple of times and then handed me three twenty dollar bills.

"I do," he slurred.

Jerry, I realized, was drunk enough to give *me* money. I knew this because before I had even left the bar with Patti, he had forsaken the utility of a mug and was drinking, two-handed, straight out of the pitcher.

MONEY.

He had saved me, sort of.

The next morning, Nikki and I set out bright and early at noon to begin the treasure hunt for my car. We got the address of the towing company off of the sign in front of 6 East and headed down McClintock to reclaim it with Jerry's money in my pocket.

We drove up and down that street seven goddamn times before we realized that the address was imaginary and entirely non-existent. There was no such place. It was at this point that I changed my mind about the most cruel creatures on this earth, credit collectors, and moved them to second place on my "People Who Are So Evil I Would Never Even Date One" list and plopped towing people straight at number one.

The night before I was mad, by the morning I became angry but now I was furious, and Nikki was so hung over she couldn't even smoke.

"I hope those people had to get in my car and drive it," I screamed. "I hope that when they were in there, cigarette butts flew up and hit them in the face. I hope they cut their feet when they stepped on the beer bottles and I hope they stuck their hands in what's left of Doug's vomit!"

We finally went to my friend Kate's house to call the tow people. Nikki had to do it, I was too upset. She dialed the number, lying down, and I paced around the room.

The phone rang, and rang, and rang, and finally someone answered.

"Do you have Laurie's car?" she asked them right away. "She wants it back. Okay. Hang on. Laurie, what's your license plate number?"

"I don't know!" I answered. "You just tell them it's the car that has a purple Stretch Armstrong doll in the back window, leaking all of its innards. That shouldn't be too hard to find!"

"There's a doll in the back window," Nikki relayed. "It's purple and it's bleeding."

"Do a shot, Laurie," Kate said. "It will relax you a little bit."

"Oh no!" I replied. "I'll lose my edge if I do that. I want to keep my edge; I need to keep my edge because I'm going to go in there crazy. *Crazy. Kate.* I'm so goddamned pissed off that I think I just may take hostages."

"WHAT?" I heard Nikki yell. "We have to make an *appointment?* An *appointment?* We have to have an appointment to get her car?"

"GIVE ME THAT PHONE," I roared, and ripped it out of Nikki's hand. "Now you listen to me," I started. "I want my car back NOW. What the hell do you mean I have to make an appointment? You are not a beauty salon, *I'm not calling to get my damn nails done!*"

"I'm just the answering service, ma'am," the voice on the other line said. "Be down at the towing yard at two."

Then she gave me the real and secret address for TowAmerica, which is **808 SOUTH McCLINTOCK,** (so in case these bastards ever tow your car, you don't have to waste any time looking for a fake address and you can go down right away, armed. I would have had better luck trying to find Salmon Rushdie or the Honeycomb Hideout than this place) I threw down the phone and then wished so badly that I had been born a gypsy or in Haiti so that I could practice nasty voodoo curses.

Nikki and I arrived at TowAmerica at 1:45 so we could stake the place out before the rendezvous. We spotted my car, way back in the lot, and it was at this point that Nikki turned to me.

"Do you still have your edge?" she asked me. "Because this damn gate is open. It's not locked. I'm feeling invincible and I'm not even drunk. Let's steal your car back!"

"Hell yes! Are your warrants cleared up yet?" I said, and she shook her head. "Okay, then you stay here and hold the gate. I'm going in."

"What if there are dogs?" she asked.

I held up my weapon. "Chili powder spray," I replied. "I've sprayed myself with this shit and remained blind for forty-five minutes, remember? Believe me, I know it works."

"What if they have cameras?"

I unabashedly shrugged.

"You know, they stole it from me, like pirates, I'm just stealing it back. Eye for an eye, car for a car. Pirate for a pirate!"

I was shaking, and I was nervous. Believe it or not, I've never been arrested before, but I thought, WHAT WOULD JANIS HAVE DONE, and you're damn right, she would have stolen her car back and that's exactly what I was going to do. And that's what I was thinking as I grabbed my keys and Nikki The Accomplice held the gate open, that's what I was thinking as I was about to place my first step inside the yard, ready to spray the dogs, that's what I was thinking just as a huge yellow tow truck pulled up into the parking lot of TowAmerica and the driver turned and smiled at us.

"Oh shit!" Nikki exclaimed in a whisper. "Oh shit! Laurie that's the tow man, did you see him! Oh God, that's him! He's nice! And he's cute! Oh shit!"

So yes, I forked over Jerry's money, now damp and sweaty, to the cute tow man with the nice smile, he showed me to my car and held the gate open as Nikki and I drove through. The edge had been scared shitless right out of me, so bad that I couldn't even say one single mean thing to him.

"Have a nice day," he said as he waved to us on the way out.

I stopped the car. I had to say *something*.

"You ever read the State Press at ASU?" I asked him.

"Yeah, sure," he nodded. "Sometimes I pick it up."

"I suggest you pick it up on Thursday," I added. "This Thursday. And look for the same name you have on my receipt."

"Okay," he smiled.

"You know what else?" I continued.

"What's that?" he replied.

"Never in a million years would I ever date you," I said, before I punched the gas again and turned onto McClintock, driving in my own damn car.

Fat Head

When I walked into the State Press newsroom last Thursday morning, the day had already begun to take shape nicely. I didn't have a hangover, my dogs hadn't defecated on my kitchen floor and I got to yell at two blonde women in traffic, *on two separate occasions.*

Needless to say, I was looking forward to what the day had to deliver when the newsroom suddenly hushed when I arrived, and the regular bustle was replaced with darting whispers.

"Do you think she's seen it?"

"Where is it?"

"She's smiling. I don't think she's seen it."

"She's going to have a fit. I know she's going to have a fit."

"When she sees it, she's gonna hit somebody."

"Oh God. She hasn't seen it."

Everybody was staring at me, and I knew it was bad. My friend Kris came forth and took me by the shoulders. She only does this when she knows I'm going to hit somebody.

"How bad is it?" I squeaked.

"Sit down," she said, and guided me to the closest chair. She looked me in the eye. "Now I want you to be calm, and to try to act as professional as possible. People are watching."

I nodded.

"It's the Blue Copy," she said.

The Blue Copy is a copy of the State Press that our advisor, Bruce, looks over every day and writes down his criticisms and comments on and then gives back to us to plug up the holes in our souls and self-worth when we read it.

Kris turned to the page with my column on it and handed it to me.

"I got this far this time," Bruce wrote, indicating a line underneath the first paragraph. "I sure do wish you'd write about something other than yourself."

I was trying to compose myself, trying to remember that a couple of days ago one of the discs in his back turned to dust due to the aging process so he had to be driven around to all of the classes that he teaches in a golf cart and that he is in severe anguish and that he needs desperately to take it out on someone when I saw his last comment, scribbled in teeny little letters on the bottom of the page: "And don't get a fat head."

FAT HEAD. Write something about something besides *myself*? Is there someone else who will let me follow them around when they're drunk so I can document all the stupid things they do?

But then, after a day or so, I thought, "Bruce is right. Maybe people are getting sick of me. Take a break. Ease up. Humiliate someone else for a change."

So there we have it. Instead of writing about FAT HEAD this week, I'm going to write about my FAT HEAD FAMILY and my FAT

HEAD FRIENDS. FAT HEAD FAMILY AND
FREINDS FACTS:

My Aunt Adele, who is my favorite aunt
in the world because she's *just like me*, had
horrible, painful headaches so she went to the
doctor and when she was sitting in the doctor's
waiting room, a picture fell off the wall and hit
her in the head so she sued him and won *three
thousand dollars*.

That's a fact.

My identical twin cousins, Matt and
Mike, personally met and lived with Timothy
Leary in the late sixties and used such an
abundance of LSD that their brains were
reduced to the mental capacity of sponge cake.
Mike was committed to a very nasty New York
state hospital in 1971, and once when Matt went
to visit him, (try to follow me on this one) Mike
convinced the guards that he was Matt while
Matt was in the bathroom, resulting in Matt's
incarceration despite his feeble protests and
Mike's newfound freedom. Matt remained in the
hospital for six months until Mike was found in
Upstate New York, lying in the middle of some
road under a pile of leaves in the dead of winter,
naked as the day both him and Matt were born.

That's a fact.

Matt, after he was released from the
hospital, immigrated to Phoenix via cattle cars
and arrived at my family's house at three o'clock

in the morning with a nickel and a matchbook in his pocket.

During dinner the next night, he had a flashback and began to sing "Smoke On the Water," I did not recognize at the time as being one of The Holy Trinity Of Rock Songs. I was only eleven.

Anyway, groovy cat Matt moved downtown and burglarized a couple of houses, and in one of the burglaries he strangled the family cat. When my father asked him why he did this, he explained that he was hallucinating and thought the cat was a lion.

Matt now lives somewhere near Los Angeles in a cave, and drops us postcards in between hallucinations. He also once worked for Kentucky Fried Chicken but never for the Post Office.

That's a fact.

My grandfather, who we call Pop Pop, is a very thrifty man and has devoted his life since 1972 to make grocery shopping a game as well as a hobby. At last count, there were 34 cans of sauerkraut and an equal amount of fruit cocktail in his pantry that is dangerously close to expiring. It keeps him busy and we love him for it.

Sometimes, though, Pop Pop gets carried away with what he thinks is a good deal. A good example of this is when my mother, two sisters and I went to my grandparents' house for a visit.

Pop Pop was very excited and said he had a rare treat for all of us, that we were to share equally and not fight over it, that there was enough for everyone and not to be stingy. He disappeared to Food Storage Unit #3 and came back with two huge boxes, placing them gently on the table and backed away to watch the expressions of bliss on our faces bloom.

We opened them slowly, hoping it was candy or a Barbie RV or thousands of Bonnie Bell Lip Smackers. The lids unfolded, like the petals of a flower, to reveal a lot, if not a case, of Jheri Curl.

"It's for your hair," he said, smiling from the corner. "They had a whole table of them at Walgreens," and then offered to go back and buy the *rest*.

That's a fact.

I have a friend named Colleen. She is addicted to *Beverly Hills, 90210*, and Laurie is not allowed to call her when the show is on. Colleen cried with happiness when the two-hour episode was on, and once when I was having a crisis last week and Colleen *did* pick up the phone, Colleen interrupted and said hysterically, "Laurie, I have to go. *Dylan is picking.*"

After Dylan picked Kelly instead of Brenda, Colleen constructed a shrine to Brenda out of a shoe box, complete with the Brenda doll Laurie bought her for Christmas, candles and fruit offerings. The Brenda doll has a picture of

Kelly in her hand with a skull drawn over it. Colleen refuses to disassemble the shrine until Brenda has been vindicated. I've had to tell her, "Let Brenda's pain be Brenda's pain," but Colleen won't listen.

I am especially worried because Colleen keeps telling her that she's "going to Donna's house," when in reality she doesn't even *know* anyone named Donna.

That's a scary fact.

Then there's Gene, my endearing and beloved friend, who, when he drinks, always has mixer left over and no alcohol, and who is also prone, while in this state, to leave messages on answering machines of the sort, "I have four words for you. Canadian Mist will f---- you up."

Gene is convinced that his destiny lies in an aluminum sided mobile home in Casa Grande, swigging bourbon straight from the bottle and dying while watching a Gene Hackman movie in a room lit only by one bare bulb swinging back and forth. He was at my Halloween birthday party this year dressed as a "desperate realtor."

Ask Gene, that's a fact.

So there you have it, Bruce.

FAT HEAD yourself.

Sprung and Broken

Sun tan oil. Bikinis. Volleyball. The beach. Sand in your crotch.

Spring Break.

Count me out.

When my friend Jamie suggested that we go somewhere for spring break last year, I was aghast.

"We don't need to go anywhere," I snapped. "We can stay home and get drunk. It's cheaper and besides, I don't want to spend a whole week waiting to get date raped."

"No," she argued, "I think we need to travel, a road trip, pack up the car, get a carton of smokes, a bag of Funyuns and we're off. It will do you good."

"Can we bring whiskey?" I inquired.

"Well, of course," she said triumphantly, and it was decided.

We were going somewhere.

"Florida?" she suggested.

"The Land of the Lost Senior Citizens? No thank you. We could have fun with microwaves down there, although the chance of competing in one of those inner-fulfilling, non-sexist, personally rewarding wet T-shirt contests seems mighty appetizing."

"Mazatlan?" she offered.

I just looked at her. Evidently, she had very high hopes for this trip, and she was acting as if we both still had credit cards that worked. One by one, the plastic golden keys to our life of luxury were seized at inopportune times, ripped apart in front of our eyes in various restaurants and department stores. We screamed and wept in horror as if they were our children.

Now we were operating on a cash only basis, which limited our options tremendously. It had to be cheap. It had to be within a reasonable driving distance. She wanted to be near a beach. This left us only one choice: Rocky Point, Mexico, also known as the poor man's Mazatlan. So poor, it's zoned as Section 8 of vacation spots.

We convinced our friend Stacy to join us because she had a tent and never went anywhere without ten packs of cigarettes. She is also the strongest girl I know and can balance a case of beer on one shoulder. She's a woman, all right. We would be safe with her.

And then we were off.

We reached the border in a matter of hours, and it was apparent that we had because the American asphalt abruptly stopped and was met with what Mexico paves their roads with, which is lava.

I thought it was very festive for Mexico to decorate the sides of the roads with little shrines and flowers, because these things are all over the place. The most frequent theme was the Virgin Mary, making it seem like Mexico is a very religious and holy land. Every hundred yards or so, the little Virgin Mary would pop her head up, and another shrine would appear.

I thought it was all a little bit funky until Stacy informed me that the shrines were actually graves and not holy decorations, and that people get buried in Mexico wherever it is that they drop dead. Just dig a hole, fill it up and crown it with a plaster of Paris Mother of God.

As soon as we made it into Rocky Point, Jamie and Stacy headed directly for the beach. As they bound into the ocean and played in the surf, I was busy in the sand building my cabana to shield me from the sun. I haven't been in direct sunlight for nearly seven years, and am convinced that my skin will begin to bubble and then fall off my bones in big, smoldering fleshy chunks if I am exposed.

Then the best thing in the world happened. A little man appeared with a basket of burritos, another popped up with a tray of silver jewelry, and yet another came forth bearing straw hats. It was Mexico's version of the Home Shopping Network, right on the beach. Bartering is still alive and thriving in Rocky Point, because I traded two Pepsis for a silver ring and was very proud of myself for making such a deal until two weeks later when my finger turned green and swelled up like a sausage and my father had to cut the damn thing off my finger with a pair of hedge clippers.

After a while, it had become clear to me that I needed to use the rest room and I looked around, but couldn't find anything that resembled one. I walked down towards the water where Stacy and Jamie were swimming. I ventured in, getting my ankles wet, and then went in up to my knees.

"Hey, you guys," I yelled when they were close enough to hear me, "Where's the bathroom?"

Stacy started to laugh, and then screamed out, "You're standing in it!"

It seems that the beauty of going to the beach is not the silky, warm sand between your toes, or the splash of the surf against the shore, or the shadow of sea gulls flying against a fiery horizon. No, the beauty of going to the beach is that you can take a piss in the ocean whenever you feel like it, because apparently everyone does it. It's just one giant aquarium without a filter.

During the next three days, we drank whiskey, smoked, ate what the peddlers brought us on the beach, peed in the ocean and never, at any time, did we meet one single man with a full set of teeth that he couldn't pull out of his mouth with the mere suction of his tongue.

It probably would have been the same thing in Florida.

Rusty, The Pit to Hell and the Makings of a Tramp

I was doing what I do best, smoking a cigarette, drinking a Pepsi and talking on the phone to my friend Colleen. We were discussing the boundaries of the number of people any person could sleep with in a year before being considered a tramp.

The doorbell rang. I had to put the phone down, get off my phone stool and answer it. On the other side of the door was a round, pudgy, bearded man. He was smiling, a full smile minus a front tooth or so.

"Hi!" he said, rather cheerily.

"Hi. I'm on the phone," I said, rather irritably.

"Oh, well, I'm from AT & T," he informed me.

I got the nervous hot flash and I was stunned for a second from fear.

"Oh my God, you're not shutting it off again, are you?" I cried. "I've been really good about paying the bill this time. I won't let you shut it off. Go away. Or can hang out on the porch as long as you want to because I'm not letting you get near my phone."

You must understand that the phone is very important to me. I cannot exist with out it. I have to call Colleen every time something happens to me, which is all the time. Before I get out of bed in the morning I call people, because the phone does not rest on a dresser or night table. The phone sleeps in the bed with me.

Of course, this poses a delicate problem from callers that do not adhere to the Twelve O'Clock Rule. The Twelve O'Clock Rule is a commandment instituted by very wise people that stay out late and need sleep. Nobody that I know is allowed to call me before noon, and I, in turn, am not allowed to call anybody else before noon. It is illegal for anybody to break this rule, but my mother and creditors do it all the time.

"Too much sleep will make you sick," my mother says. "Now get up and clean your house. It's filthy."

Anyway, the fat little man chuckled. His name patch said "Rusty" in red script letters. "No, no, no. We're not shutting off your phone. We're putting in some new copper wire that will make you hear conversations crisper and cleaner," Rusty said, waving around his fat midget arms. His fingernails were framed in black tarry stuff. "You will be amazed at how sharp the sound will be. The only thing is, we need to dig a little bitty hole in your yard. Nothing big, just a hole, say-oh, I don't know, couple feet deep, couple feet across, you know. Nothing big. Do we have your permission?"

"Sure," I said, ecstatic that my phone was still useable without having to pay three months' worth of delinquent bills and another deposit. "Dig as much as you want." Rusty told me that they would start on Monday.

What Rusty did not tell me was to park my car elsewhere, like in New Mexico, because when Monday morning rolled around, an army of farm equipment chugged down the street and parked anywhere they damn well pleased, including in front of my driveway.

I went out to my car, got in and started to back up, only to find that if I attempted to get out, I would have sodomized my car with a backhoe. I was trapped.

I was angry, but I was sure that I could easily resolve the situation with a little bit of feminine charm, because a little bit is all I have, and the ability to reason. I tracked Rusty down to the spigot in my front yard, where he had thrust a dirty old green garden hose down his throat and was hastily gulping water.

"Rusty," I said with a smile, "I need to get out of my driveway to go to school. Can anyone move that big yellow thing from the sidewalk?"

"Well, Nelson's driving the backhoe, and he's on a break, so it'll be a while," he said, wiping this mouth with his shirt. Rusty had the biggest belly I had ever seen. I was stunned. It was so big that he had to run his belt underneath his cargo because the girth of it was just too big. He had stretch marks, too.

"Can you go and get him?" I said. "I need to go now."

"Well, Nelson usually sleeps in the cab during breaks, but I'll try to get him up."

I was wondering what Nelson was on a break *from*. Nothing had been dug up yet, nothing was marked. I thought they'd better hurry up if they were going to be done by tonight.

Nelson begrudgingly moved the backhoe and then spit in my driveway when he was done.

When I came home, I looked at my front yard and realized that they had done such a good job digging that hole in my yard that you couldn't even tell. Everything looked just like it had before. I was amazed.

Until the next morning. I went out to go to work, the street was clogged with monstrous yellow pieces of machinery and the backhoe was blocking me in again.

I knew where to find Rusty this time. He was sitting underneath a tree in the front yard, eating Sno Balls.

"Rusty," I said, a little impatient this time, "Get Nelson up right now. I have to go to work." We repeated the procedure again, and again Nelson spit in the driveway.

That night when I came home, it looked like a carnival was going on in the street. In front of my house. In my yard.

Placed strategically to cause the most commotion possible, flags, lights and barricades overtook the part where the sidewalk used to be, the part where my fence used to be, and the part where my yard used to be.

I literally had no yard left. What they had done to my lawn forced them to put up a sign, with lights, of course, that screamed, "Street Closed."

The fence in my front yard was gone, now placed on the side of the house like a bundle of toothpicks. I peeked over the lines of flags at the hole in my yard. It went down, down, down, so far down I couldn't see the bottom. It wasn't a couple of feet wide, either, like Rusty had promised. It was more like ten or eleven. The AT & T people were digging a pool in my yard.

Just then, Rusty pulled up in a tractor. "Morning, Laurie," he said.

"Rusty, this is not a little hole," I said. "This could easily be a Nazi bunker."

He nodded as he looked in the hole like construction people are trained to do. "Yeah, yeah, it's a good size hole, but in a couple of days you won't even know we've been here," Rusty said.

A couple of days turned into three months. Rusty sat in what was left of my yard so often that he earned Squatter's Rights. So did the rest of the crew, who were so busy guarding the "Street Closed" sign and waving traffic flags at moving cars that they really didn't have time to dig or fill up the hole. A couple of times, the crew had vanished even though their equipment remained. I knew where they were. They were in the hole. It had become a clubhouse of sorts.

One day I prayed and the next morning I woke up and God had given me a sidewalk. It was a small step, I knew, but it was a start. It was something. I decided to pray harder the next night, burn candles or drink holy water or whatever in order to get my yard back.

The next morning I woke up in an earthquake. The windows were rattling, the bed was shaking, and the world was crumbling. I ran to the window, and, with the sunrise behind him like a bad western painting, Nelson and his trusty backhoe were chopping up the street like an onion. And he didn't stop with the street. He went for the sidewalk, too.

"No! Nelson, no!" I screamed. "Not the sidewalk! I just got it!" and I was sad until I looked at the clock and saw it was six o'clock in the morning and then I got really mad. The Twelve O'clock Rule had been broken, dammitt, and I decided to break all of hell loose myself.

I situated myself on my phone stool, leafed through the phone book and called AT & T. I reached a perky operator by the name of Mary who was nice to me for the first three seconds of the phone call.

"Mary, and there is a crew in my front yard, a troop of bulldozers that are headed for my bedroom wall," I said. "I want you to make them stop."

"Evidently, ma'am, you don't understand that the afternoons get very hot and the crews need to make an early start," Mary sniped.

"Evidently you don't understand that it is six o'clock in the morning and I only have six hours before I have to wake up," I retorted. "I want to speak to a field manager."

"I'll leave a message but it will be at least an hour before they can call you back."

"Fine. In that case I want to file a complaint. Yes I do. I am making a complaint, do you understand? Are you writing this down?"

It did no good. Nelson was going hog wild with the asphalt, the walls were still shaking and I was awake. And defeated.

I went out to the front yard and found Rusty in his same spot, underneath a tree drinking a two-liter bottle of Big K cola.

"Morning, Laurie," he said.

"Morning, Rusty," I answered as I sat down beside him. "How many people do you think a person could sleep with in a year before they were considered a tramp?"

Permed

Everyone I know has a bad perm story.

Everyone has had their hair frizzled and fried, burnt beyond recognition and falling out in clumps. It's a story that stays with you, it doesn't go away, and pops up in nightmares, anxiety attacks when passing a corner beauty shop, or hears a song on the radio that reminds them of their tragedy.

I, for one, know that I can't hear Kajagoogoo's "Too Shy" without breaking into a cold, clammy sweat and reaching for my scalp for reassurance that the ordeal really is over. It was the early eighties, and I felt that it was time for a change. My head had been bleached, shaved, bi-leveled and dyed a myriad of colors, and I wanted to be adventurous. Sadly mistaking my natural curl for the blown-dry frizz that awful seventh-grade class pictures documented, I got a perm on a whim. I plopped my then-auburn hair into the hands of a stranger who didn't ask me any of the necessary questions (Has your hair been bleached, dyed or permed within the last six months?) and went directly to work. By the time I got home, I had an orange Afro, and when I walked into the house, my mother screamed, "Jesus Christ Almighty, what the hell did you do now?" and began to cry.

It was irreparable, even through the efforts my mother made of hot oil and deep conditioning, curl relaxer and eventually another perm to straighten my hair completely. When my hair grew out another inch, she dragged me to her stylist who shaved me like a dog, and strangers called me "Mister" for the following six months.

Why did I do it again? I don't know, I really don't. I have curly hair. But it wasn't curly enough. It was never enough. I wanted Andie McDowell hair, Elaine hair, and before I knew what had happened, I had the box in my hand last Sunday and I was writing a check.

I went home and started rolling, heat activated myself and neutralized. I unrolled. Wet, it looked okay. A little tight, but okay. It would relax in a couple of days, and the smell of perm, otherwise known as a combination of the underside of Satan's hoof and a nuclear reactor meltdown, ran off to the store to buy dog food, and as I passed the glass of the meat counter, I peered in. I could have been the drummer in Lenny Kravitz' band.

I looked around, panicked, and what I saw scared me even more. Everyone there had the same hair as me. The woman in the flip-flops, T-shirt and no bra. The girl with the jeans slung off her ass and the teardrop tattoo next to her eye. The cashiers, although their bangs stood straight up.

Oh my God, I whimpered, my had flying to my mouth. I had gang girl hair!!

Memory served me well as I saw flashes of my Bozo the Clown hair fifteen years ago. Another perm!, I thought as I raced past shampoos and deodorant. I have to straighten this out immediately!

At home, I applied the heat activation again, and with a comb, straightened and straightened and straightened until I was sure my gang girl hair was gone. When my husband came home an hour later, I didn't have to say anything.

"What happened to your hair?" he asked quizzically, touching the ends of my hair lightly. "You look like one of those corn-husk dolls."

"It's a perm," I said quietly.

"I don't think perms are supposed to do that," he said. "Your hair's kind of shaped like a triangle, with the ends flared out. Perms are supposed to be curly."

"Well," I answered briefly, "The first one was."

The next day, I woke up with a sick feeling, a deep, dark, heavy feeling, the same kind of feeling I usually have after I crash one of my dad's cars. I couldn't understand why, until I looked in the mirror. I had a scarecrow head. It looked like straw; straight, lifeless, ready to be sheared off of my head and woven into a basket.

No hat, scarf or barrette was going to cover this. I called my friend Laura in New York, who had also just gotten fried. I felt better calling her because she had paid $70 for her disaster.

"Okay," she snapped sharply, gearing into combat mode. "Go right now to Neiman

Marcus and buy this conditioner, then buy this kind of gel. Get a diffuser for your hairdryer; you're going to need it. Get some sculpting mud from this salon in Scottsdale. Start using this kind of shampoo. Wear your hair up as much as you can. Time is the only thing that can solve this. You need to heal. Let yourself cry. Do you still have the number to your old therapist?"

I needed people who understood. I called everyone I knew that had been frizzed, and they all offered advice, kind words and...even hope.

And when I finally got into see my therapist, I arrived just as her last patient was leaving, her puffy, red eyes turned downward, her lip trembling, her feet shuffling. All the trademarks of someone in real distress. My first thought was a hoarder, someone dealing with addiction, the shame of a sex worker, but I had no idea just how bad it was until I passed her and detected the commingled notes of Satan's hoof and the traces of a nuclear reactor melted like a candle.

Stroked Out

It was a really really hot summer day and I was getting ready to zoom to the bank to cover a hot check. I was rushed, it was an emergency. I opened the carport door, walked outside, turned the lock on the handle and shut the door.

I went for my key ring, always conveniently located somewhere in the bottomless pit I carry on my shoulder. I searched through pocket one: Nothing but a Juicy Fruit wrapper and a little knob of a pretzel. Onto pocket two: Nothing but a handful of tobacco flakes, three pennies and a coupon for 25 cents off of Vani-Flush. Pocket three: (Panic sets in. My face gets hot, I start to shake a little and I get that stabbing cramp in my stomach that I get when I know I've broken something beyond measure.) The sizzling checkbook that got me into this mess in the first place, a broken pen oozing ink and a birthday card, now dirty and frayed, that I never sent to my grandmother.

No Keys.

For an ordinary person, this would not usually pose that great of a problem. But for me, #1) I don't live with my parents anymore, they live thirteen houses away so I am alone and lost in this whirlpool of tragedy; #2) It is 110 degrees and I have not one cigarette; and, finally and most importantly, #3) I live in a house where paranoia was previously an occupant. There are bars on the windows, bars on the doors, and bars, very much like those at Buckingham Palace to keep the masses away, but these are for rapists, that close the opening and sides of the carport and can only be opened with a key, the very same key that is sitting on the counter in my kitchen, which is, in reality, only two feet away from me.

I cannot get out of the carport and I cannot get into the house. I am trapped.

I try a variety of methods to save myself. I scream for my neighbor, Carol, whom I know is home because she works the evening shift at MegaFoods and her car is in the driveway. "CAAAARROOOOLLLL!!!!!!" But she doesn't answer.

I measure the teeny opening at the top of the gate, and figure that if I stand on the trunk of my car, leap onto the gate and can fit my head through the passage, I can hoist myself over and fall to freedom on the other side. The only problem with this plan of action is my butt, which, for caloric and girth reasons, is bigger than my head.

I decide to go for it. I stand on the trunk at jump onto the gate, but it swings a little and I am afraid that the hinges will burst out of the wall, but I lose my balance anyway and fall back on the ground, knocking the wind out of my lungs and hyperventilating.

I summon a passerby, a lady power walker, from the other side of the street.

"Hey lady!" I scream, still hoarse from screaming for Carol. "Hey lady would you help me please?"

She crosses the street, ventures up my driveway but stops about ten feet away from the gate so that I can't bite her.

"Are you in some kind of...trouble?" she says. (She is old.)

I am in the middle of explaining my situation when who but my sister drives by. Right in front of my house. Doesn't even look at my house. Not a glance.

"LADY THAT IS MY SISTER THAT'S MY SISTER GO GET HER QUICK," I say, because there is a stop sign at the end of my block which is good for at least a five-second lapse time knowing how my sister obeys traffic laws.

The lady looks at me. Then the freak runs out onto the middle of the road, stops on the pavement and says to me, if you can believe this, "Where do you think she's going?"

Where do I think she is going.

The five-second edge we once had is now gone, and my sister continues on her journey.

Big salty pools of tears well in my eyes and I answer her in a cracked whisper, "I do not know."

I was going to die in my carport, alone, thirsty, hungry and needing to go potty. I was going to die like an animal in a cage, with just an inch of metal separating me from freedom and the comfort of my own bathroom.

The lady power walker waddles away, striding off down the street, offended at something I may have called her.

Two hours later, my neighbor Bill drove up, I called to him right away, but he couldn't figure out where the voice was coming from and was looking around the bushes in his front yard. This is a man that took strategic care of his front yard and tended the lone pine tree, the centerpiece, like it was a premature baby until one day he got into a fight with his wife and he marched his 100-pound body out to the front yard with an ax in his hand and swung at that tree until it looked like a giant pencil sticking out of the dirt.

So it did not surprise me that I was going to have to yell out directions for Bill to be able to see me, and I did note a spark of disappointment in his eye when he realized it was me. He sauntered across the street, his hands in his pockets as if he sees his neighbor trapped like an elephant behind bars pretty much every day. Then he asked me what happened, I told him, and he nodded.

"Could you please call my mom?" I pleaded.
"She has the keys and I wrote her a bad check."

Bill agreed and sauntered back across the street. But then he doesn't come back. He doesn't do anything; not tell me if rescue is on the way, not if the line is busy, or if there was no answer, or if my mom already knows that the check I wrote her was bad.

He just left me there.

Finally, after about twenty minutes, my mother drove up, got out of the car and threw the key at me with the word, "jackass." The rules in my family have now changed so that when anyone ever leaves my parents' house, they have to drive by mine to see if I'm trapped inside my own carport again.

I never saw the lady power walker after that. But sometimes, when I watch Bill watering his lawn and looking forlornly at the spot where the giant pencil used to be, I know he's listening, listening closely, just in case the bushes say something again.

Lordy Lordy Lordy

He wasn't my type.

He didn't look like he smoked, his hair was short and apparently clean, and his clothes were sporty and appeared first-hand.

He didn't seem like he had ever been to jail.

159

It was the first day of freshly born semester; he walked into the classroom that housed Italian 101 and stood awkwardly near the front, shifting his weight nervously from foot to foot.

Come sit by me, the sexy baby voice in my head whispered, *come sit by me.* I tried with my mind powers to hypnotize him to draw him to me like a magnet, steadily staring at him the whole time to make my ESP talent work even better. In simply an instant, I knew he was mine. My Mate. My Missing Half.

But he remained at the front of the room, scanning the faces of the other students until the bell rang. Still, he did not sit down but continued to lean up against the wall, not making a move.

Then he cleared his throat.

Oh no.

Silence soaked the room.

No, no, no, I thought.

"Hello," he announced.

Please, God, I begged, please just let him be some random jackass that's lost or schizophrenic, I can handle schizophrenia, too, but I cannot handle the fact that the man that I love is probably my teacher.

"I am Luigi," he proclaimed in a thick Italian accent. "I am your professor."

GOD DAMMIT! the sexy voice wailed, this brutal world is so unfair! Is this what you want from me, God, a man that will be forced to give me a grade?

Realizing the immanent tragedy, I extinguished my ESP powers and tried not to pay Luigi any unnecessary attention, and kept my head up to stretch out the skin bridge between my neck and chin.

I did this for weeks, *weeks,* until the day that I failed the first test.

Luigi told me to come by after class, and of course, I did, fully aware that I was playing with matches in a mobile home while wearing highly combustible pajamas. I checked to make sure I had no lipstick on my teeth. I approached his desk.

He turned around.

I smiled.

He smiled.

"You have failed the test," he said. "That is not good."

I nodded. I figured that if I didn't say anything, there wouldn't be any chance of me spitting on him accidentally while I talked.

"You must study harder."

I nodded again.

"Come to the study group. We will meet at the coffee house tomorrow at one o'clock."

I nodded.

When I saw him the next day, he sat alone, relaxed in a white chair, dressed in pressed white shorts and a wrinkle-free white shirt. He was sipping espresso.

How can I love this man, I asked myself. *He doesn't even have a drug problem.*

"Where is the rest of the group?" I asked.

He waved his hand.

"There is no one but you and me," he said.

Uh oh, I thought. Ding! Ding! Warning bells!

Espresso. White attire. Italian accent.

The Lair Of Luigi.

"Have you eaten?" he asked. "I know of this place that has good pizza. The best pizza. *Gooood* pizza."

Well, I'm always hungry, and I figured that he must know what he's talking about, I mean, he was Italian, *Italian* Italian, he must know *gooood* pizza when he sees it.

"Sure," I answered. "Pizza sounds good. Do you want me to drive?"

He laughed.

"No. We will walk. It is not far."

So we started to walk, and we walked, and we walked, and we walked, we walked two miles to get to Luigi's fantastic pizza place, we walked for an hour until we were standing right smack in front of Pizza Hut.

Ding! Ding!

I said nothing.

Luigi ordered a large pizza with everything on it, every possible animal by-product and every vegetable cultivated on this continent.

It was then that he told me how he could never spend the rest of his life with one woman; his soul was too big for that. He needed many different experiences, with many different women, to feed the hunger in his heart. He said he even found his sister attractive. He had too much love to give to just one person; he felt he had to spread it around.

It's not love that this guy wants to spread around, the sexy voice said in my head as it turned angry. The only things he wants to spread will not have my tights coming off of them.

Then the pizza came, steaming and hot, and Luigi lunged at it like a prisoner. Before I was able to even lift one piece onto my plate, he had wolfed down two, and wolfed down is the correct term because I have never seen any mammal eat in that manner except in documentaries. He consumed the pizza without the art of chewing, he just bit and swallowed, bit and swallowed, much like the way a dog eats a raw piece of meat. Pieces of bell pepper flew onto my plate, along with a mangled black olive. I needed the salt but was too afraid to reach for it, should my fingers arrive in any area of his eating boundary, get tangled in the feeding frenzy.

It was obscene. He consumed the remaining eight pieces in the same way, and when he was done, a circle of pizza sauce illuminated his mouth and he smiled. He had sausage in his teeth.

"Are you ready to go?" I asked him. "Or did you want devour the family of four sitting behind us?"

I had thought about preparing for the three-hour hike back to my car, and had speculated that it would be in my best interest to bring food rations and a couple of gallons of water. The water, as it turned out, was going to be redundant, since a torrential rainstorm had moved in and exploded with raindrops so big they hurt when they hit you.

By the time we had made it halfway, water was running down my face in streams, my hair hung in clumps and the pretty little outfit I was wearing clung to me like I was a marshmallow that had been vacuum-sealed.

We were trying to walk fast, I don't know why, I wasn't going to get any dryer and I couldn't have gotten any wetter.

"Faster, faster!" Luigi shouted as his hairy little Italian legs almost burst into a run, "Faster!" and then, all of a sudden, he screamed like a woman and doubled over, clutching his abdomen.

"What's wrong?" I asked, even though I was pretending care.

"Clamps!" he expressed through clenched teeth, "Clamps!"

"What the hell are you talking about, *Clamps?*" I responded. "What do you need clamps for? Are you diabetic? Is it a diabetic thing?"

He shook his head and wailed, "CLAMPS!"

Whatever, I thought, I can't understand you damn foreigners.

"*English!*" I shouted. "Tell me in *English! I can't speak Italian, remember? I failed the test!*"

Then he pointed to his stomach, and I realized he was trying to tell me that he had *cramps*, clearly a result of gluttony, the inability to masticate and the sin pain God was stabbing him with because of what he said about his sister. He had eaten too much and then tried to *run*.

"Well, no wonder," I said to him. "You'd better get up, because in a minute we're going to have to *swim* back to the car."

Finally, after about a half an hour, Luigi straightened up and was able to walk without screaming in agony and we made it to the car. I decided to be nice and give him a ride to his bike, an offer he gladly accepted.

I put the car in drive and pressed the gas pedal, and the car began bucking like a low rider on a Saturday night. Suddenly the car lurched forward and then catapulted, catching a wee bit of hair until it finally made contact with the asphalt again.

"Lordy Lordy Lordy!" Luigi shrieked, but I could tell him that was a wasted effort. Once you vocalize that you want to diddle your sister, God is no longer taking calls from you.

I lost control of the car; it drove itself out of the street and onto the sidewalk, where it spun through the grass of a park before I hit the brakes. We screeched to a halt with an ear-piercing squeal that was either the tires or Luigi, I could never be sure.

In the moments of quiet that settled after, I realized I had driven over several concrete parking bumpers in the parking lot; it was dark, it was raining and I was confused and just didn't understand what was going on at all. As Mr. Toad's Wild Ride was about to end, Luigi wasted no time and leapt out of the vehicle.

"Ciao, Lordy!" he screamed over his shoulder as he scrambled off into the night.

That semester, well, I failed Italian.

What the hell did I want?

Like I said, he just *wasn't* my type.

The Melancholy Ode to Little Dog

I wasn't home for ten minutes from my vacation when my sister called and asked if I had seen the new grey cat that was hanging around the house.

"Isn't he cute?" she said.

"Yes." I said.

"Are you going to keep him?"

"No." I said.

"I'm coming over," she said.

So she comes over. She finds the cat and calls for me to come outside to show me just how much I need to keep him.

"He's got green eyes," says my sister the cat saleswoman.

"I know," I replied.

"And six toes on each paw," she said, displaying his selling point of extra phalanges. Yep. There were six.

"You keep him," I told her.

"Will you keep him for me? Please?" And in an instant after that, I had another cat.

Then BINK! this little dog just appeared, like in *Bewitched*. He wagged his tail and smiled. He would not leave. "Go away, little dog," I said, trying to push him off my porch. "Go home." He would not move. Little Dog, it seemed, *was* home.

So in approximately four minutes and a couple of seconds, I had multiplied the members of my family by 50%. I think. I live by myself, and now that I was an animal hoarder, it was probably going to stay that way.

So I let Little Dog inside. The very first thing he did when he got there was throw up on the carpet. I cleaned it up. Then he lifted his little leg as high as it would go and peed on the side of my couch. I cleaned that up, too. Then Little Dog spotted one of my original cats, since I have been collecting then now like they were something McDonald's gives out with a Cat

Lady meal, and chased it from one side of the room to the other, knocking two pictures off of the wall, pushing over a lamp, crashing a picture frame to the floor, pulling down the curtains and the rod, and finally, turning over the coffee table.

I tried in vain to find Little Dog's family. I taped 100 fliers to telephone poles, put an ad in the newspaper and walked the dog around the neighborhood, knocking on doors. No one knew of Little Dog, and had never seen him before. Little Dog was not claimed. He had no kin.

My bully dogs picked on Little Dog, so I let him sleep in my room at night. He loved to be under the covers, and would sleep on his back with his paws in the air. He snored, making pig grunts, but that didn't bother me much. I would just put the covers over his head. Little Dog had his own pillow.

Little Dog couldn't eat normal dog chow because it was too crunchy and one of his teeth fell out. So he ate Cycle Senior in a can, but it gave him some intestinal distress that caused "zipper sounds," which released a canon ball of aroma that required the evacuation of any living thing to the next room. Or outside.

He loved to bark, because he was a "Yip-Yip" dog, the kind of dog that barks at leaves, cars, and paper. He'd bark at anything.

After a couple of days, my dogs started to like Little Dog, just like I did. Little Dog got confused though, when my girl dog, Chelsea, was playing with him, biting his ears and chasing him around. Little Dog took this playfulness as amorous love, and tried to pull out his lipstick to impress her. It didn't. I guess Little Dog just loved everybody.

Little Dog even got a little used to the cats, and didn't try to bite them in the throat every time he saw them. I still had a hard time getting the cats down from the top shelf in the closet, though. Little Dog sure was a part of the family now.

I had Little Dog for two weeks when I got the message on the answering machine.

"Hi," the voice said. It was a strange voice. "My name is Scott and I saw your ad . . . and I think you might have my dog, I hope you have my dog. I'll wait for your call." And then he left a number.

I looked at Little Dog. He was outside, sniffing Chelsea's butt and getting frisky and taking the cap off of his "accessory."

And then I called the number and asked for Scott.

He described Little Dog, even down to the little red anchors woven into his collar and his missing teeth. Little Dog's real name was Gumby, and he came running right away when I called him that.

Scott drove up ten minutes later. Little Dog couldn't let a good thing go unnoticed and he chased the cat up into the closet one more time. I couldn't tell if Little Dog was especially happy to see Scott, because Little Dog was always happy, even as he climbed up into the front seat of Scott's car and then as they drove away.

I wrote a poem about Little Dog. I will tell it to you now.

THE ODE TO LITTLE DOG

Little Dog, Little Dog,
How small thou art;
Through the yips of your howls
and the poots of your farts.
I remember your grunts
When at night you would sleep,
Dreaming of cat poo
and other tasty treats.
(Note: It gets sad here.)
Oh, Little Dog, Little Dog
How much you'll be missed
As I sit on the couch
On the arm you once pissed.
You came into our home
But now you are gone
And all that remain
Are your turds on the lawn.

California License Plates

I couldn't help it.

I yelled as I hit the steering wheel for the second time, my hands balled up into little white fists.

"Goddammit, MOVE!"

The truck in front of me was leisurely slugging along, and I was late. I was already in the parking lot of the restaurant that was to host my sister's rehearsal dinner, and every single spot for as far as I could see was full. Every single spot except one.

It was on the next aisle over, sandwiched in between two sedans, and I was almost there, almost, if it wasn't for the black truck in front of me with California license plates that was blocking the necessary route that I needed to take in order to get to the spot.

I hit the steering wheel again.

"What the hell are you waiting for, huh? Do I have to get out and *push* you out of the way?"

The people driving were confused. I know this because they kept looking around as they cruised the parking lot at three miles per hour and tried to flag down other out-of-town people to ask directions.

I was late, dammit, I didn't have time to spend trapped behind bewildered tourists who had absolutely no idea what was going on in the world, or more importantly, what was going on in *my* world.

I did the only thing I could do, and that was to pull around the black truck with the imminent danger that I might sideswipe both our cars in the process. This thought popped into my mind as I saw a vision of my mother, who had told me earlier that day, "If you don't have enough respect for your sister to show up on time for the dinner, you keep this in mind: I had enough strength to bring you into this world, and I've still got enough to take you out." The notion of my mother killing me isn't what frightened me, however; it was something so much more heinous, more excruciating and irreparable than death, something so grisly and odious that I cannot say the word, I can only spell it, jay - oh - bee, because that's what I would have to get if she got pissed off enough at me for being late again and cut me off financially.

With the threat of having to work for a living, I threw the car into reverse and then back into drive, hit the gas and pulled forward just enough to be parallel to the driver's window of the black truck, saw his face melt into astonishment as I bellowed "JACKASS!" at him, flipped the corner and glided into the desired, and only, parking space.

I was pretty smug; I grabbed my purse and ran inside as fast as I could, meeting my mother at the door. She smiled. I was safe. I had gotten there on time.

We entered the patio where the dinner was already set up, nice little carafes of burgundy and Chablis on each table, the breeze was blowing slightly and the sun was getting ready to set. My sister and Taylor, her fiancée, arrived, and I waited as they took their seats at the table. I stood innocently as the guests filed in, because from here on out, I was told I *had better* exhibit **Good Behavior.** No Drinking. No Swearing. No Complaining About Being Stuck At A Non-Smoking Restaurant. No Off-Color Remarks and By God Do Not Mention The Bit About Wanting To Be A Lesbian.

I had it all down; I had memorized each and every one of the rules. I was even wearing underwear. And, just for this special occasion, I had shaved, though only up to the knees. This wasn't *my* wedding.

Then someone tapped me on the shoulder. I turned around gracefully and slowly, complete with a very polite "Yes?"

The man and woman standing before me didn't look familiar at all. They were older, a couple in their late forties, perhaps early fifties, and as my shredded little brain tried and tried, I still could not place them. It seemed like it took forever, when in reality it was only several seconds, for them to say something.

"So where did you find a parking space?" the man said, smiling.

"Excuse me?" I replied.

"Did you get that space you wanted so badly?" he asked, still smiling. "You seemed a little upset, hitting the steering wheel and all of that screaming."

"It took quite a while," I said, still not able to place these people, and I must have seemed a little confused because then the man said then, without the smile,

"I have a black truck."

And I said,

"California license plates," because then I understood, my mind flashed to that astonished look. This man was JACKASS, otherwise known as the first cousin of my sister's new father-in-law.

Embarrassed? Yes, you could say I was. Wished I had to power to vaporize myself when encountering extremely humiliating and shameful situations? That would be a fair statement. Hoped that a major vein in my head would explode to avoid having to produce my next major work of genius to try and explain myself? You betcha.

"I'm sorry," I said meekly. "I really don't want to get a job."

It had happened. I had finally outdone myself, believe it or not. I was more embarrassed than the night that I puked on the sidewalk in front of Long Wongs in front of 150 people that I knew and that knew *me*. And here I was, my sister's wedding hadn't even started yet, and I was already alienating guests and ruining her and Taylor's chances of getting a gift more glamorous than a Pyrex casserole dish.

I actually felt terrible, being that they had probably never met my sister before and my encounter with them was the first one they had had with my family. I was not setting a good example, and as the older sister, I should have gone out of my way to make sure they had a good time and that I didn't yell profanities at them, even though it was more or less provoked.

As I stood there, trying to rectify the situation, I saw he the bar was opening behind them and there were already people waiting. A line was forming.

I smiled at my sister's new cousins and said in my most polite voice, "Excuse me," but either they didn't hear me or were not done teaching me a lesson.

The line for the bar was not five people deep, then six. Seven eight nine. Within a moment, the bar was swarmed, and I lost count.

"Excuse me," I said to them again, and this time tried to get past, but they just stood there, leisurely enjoying the party and being oblivious.

Now the bar was so packed I couldn't even see it anymore, and if I didn't make it there within the next second, there was a very real possibility that I wasn't going to get what I want. Leeches that are invited to a rehearsal dinner in which my father had provided an open bar are going to drain the hard stuff first, and there way no way I wasn't going to get my fair share.

"Pardon me," I said to the cousins one more time, but they stood there like pillars of salt that had witnessed the proclivity that was going on behind me.

Two more people joined the line, then a group of three, then a bunch of my sister's friends from high school.

"GODDAMMIT, MOVE," I said to the cousins, and then I bolted.

Saddam Hussein: OS1.0

Frankly, I'm worried.

With the tenuous situation with our friend, Saddam Hussein, the world in teetering on the brink of WW III, since Boris Yeltsin, who apparently opens his day by cracking open a lime to squirt into his gin and tonic, has threatened it.

Great. Just great. This puts me in a curious position, namely because I work and live five days out of the week in Tucson, while my husband, family and dog are 100 miles away in Phoenix. I know my own luck. If a war erupts, a bomb drops on a workday, which it will, I'm stuck.

I also know my own chances--I'm five miles away from an Air Force base in Tucson (a likely target), close enough to be incinerated in the first electromagnetic wave that ripples out from ground zero. But should I survive intact, still with skin and limbs, how do I get back home? The people in Tucson are scary enough without massive exposure to radiation and anthrax for me to want to stick around.

PLAN A: I've seen The Day After, and I know how crazy people drive after bombs explode, so a car is out of the question, they'll be accidents everywhere, plus bombs kill batteries. I will have to walk. I think I can walk ten miles a day, based on the calculations of the Donner Party, since I figure that my travel:tragedy ratio would be about the same. I will need ten gallons of water, which I can either strap to my back, ankles and head unless I find an unsupervised child with a wagon (I just want the wagon, not the child). I will be mad because a war that wipes human beings off the face of the Earth will put a serious kink in my plan to become wealthy by inventing a pill that wipes out crappy songs that get stuck in your head.

PLAN B: I buy a bike, and pedal my way back home. I've ridden a stationary bike for ten minutes straight one time, but I was watching a Lindsey Wagner made-for-television movie, so this should be a realistic goal. This plan also includes an unsupervised child with a wagon which I could tie to the bike, and also provides the opportunity to carry heavier and necessary items, like Ding Dongs, a carton of cigarettes and maybe Pepsi. Upon hearing this plan, my friend Meg offered this advice: "I heard that hypnotherapy has advanced so it can really help people now." That doesn't bother me as much as the thought of "I get knocked down! And I get up again! There's no bomb that can keep me down!" circulating, reel-to-reel, in my head for the whole 100 miles because I never got my chance to do something beneficial for the world.

PLAN C: My friend, Dionne, warned me that in my physical shape, my best options are to stay put in Tucson. Since we'd probably be at work when the bomb comes, she suggested we should pick and assemble a survival pod and team of co-workers, like on Gilligan's Island. Dionne and I, of course, would be the leaders. For our pod, we picked someone with good organizational skills, another one for their camping skills (who could use one of those can openers that don't plug in) and a guy from tech support who we're pretty sure could make a ham radio out of a Mac keyboard and some paper clips. I suggested that we should also invite someone that we don't like all that much, because every organized group needs a scapegoat, and they could eventually become a food source. We figure that with our snappy personalities, girlish charm and the fact that with all of the diseases we'll have plus the likelihood that radiation will eat through our gastrointestinal organs, we'll probably lose a lot of weight and will become the most popular girls of the Nuclear World. We'll be bald and our skin will be scabby, but we're sure that our slogan of "You GLOW, girl!" will become a national anthem.

This plan, we agreed was much better than my last plan, which didn't have anything to do with biological weapons and the possibility that in several weeks' time, our intestines would most likely be hanging out of someplace nasty and start dragging on the ground. My last plan began when I thought we'd all have a lot more fun at work if we just imagined that we were all in a sitcom, but no one else heard the laugh track in their heads the way I did, and didn't understand why I would get angry when someone said something funny when we were on a commercial break.

They all thought I was crazy. They won't think so anymore when they find out they've been chosen as the scapegoat.

Goodbye, ASU

Well, I guess this is it. My last column. I'm graduating.

Well, not officially, because I got confused about how to do all the paperwork and couldn't figure it out, so I missed the deadline by a month. You people who are graduating this semester know exactly what I'm talking about. Yes, you do. It's all of the nonsense about petition forms and waiver forms and request forms and transcript forms that frame a conglomeration of perplexity so impossible to understand that it makes income tax forms look like coloring books. I'm serious. No one ever told me, "Yes, Laurie, you will go through ten years of college but will not graduate because you are not educated enough to decode the Mumbo Jumbo University Form Language to the point that you will not know where to type your name." It remains a mystery. Every time I opened the door to the room in my house large enough to hold all of these forms, my heart started pounding, my intestines churned and twisted, and I got that little knife pain in my head that makes me think I'm having an aneurism. It's the same feeling I got when someone suggested I join the State Press softball team. Right. I'd rather drink gas or get attacked by bees. I have as much of a chance of surviving a jog to first base as I do of joining a sorority. Not likely.

The one thing I really hate about my pretend graduation is that everyone, *I mean everyone,* asks me --

"So what are you doing after graduation?"

My immediate reply, of course, is, "I'm getting drunk."

Then they say, "No, I mean for real."

Then I say, "I'm getting drunk."

Then they say, "No, like for forever?"

Then I say, "Um, you mean like a *job?*"

Then they say, "Yes."

And then I say, "Hell if I know."

Because that's the truth. I have no goddamned idea.

184

I'm not skilled at anything that isn't lethal. I can't join the circus because I'm afraid of clowns. I can only type with three fingers. I don't want to work in an office unless I have my own private bathroom, because I've spent one too many years sitting in stalls waiting for the person in the next one to leave. I'm still searching for the woman with the woven leather Payless jobs that tried to outsit me for 45 minutes yesterday in Matthews Center. I will find her and then I will beat her up.

I've gone on one job interview at a newspaper. Before the interview, I went to lunch and had a sandwich with chunks of beautiful onion on it, and I love that. I didn't have any Clorets with me so I bummed a piece of gum off someone in the newsroom, a very courteous gesture on my part, I thought.

Anyway, so I sat down at this interview and I suddenly remember that I've got this piece of gum in my mouth. The interview lady is busy writing something down. I figure the only thing that I can do is try to work up enough spit in my mouth so I can swallow the gum whole. I guess I made a lot of sucking-type noises when I was doing this, and she looked and me and said, "Laurie, are you chewing gum? Because I don't talk to people who chew gum."

"No, I'm not chewing gum," I lied. "I think my tooth is coming loose and I was poking at it with my tongue." She turned away and when she wasn't looking, I spit the gum into my left hand and it stayed there, cementing my pointer finger to my palm. Then, after she had talked to me for an *entire* ten minutes, she told me that I wasn't a good listener and that I was stubborn and probably couldn't follow commands very well. She wanted me to tell her something shocking about myself, and I thought, "Whoa, this is a loaded question," and I knew I had to control myself.

"I have a dirty car," I said.

She smiled. "That's not very shocking," she quipped.

"I'm 27 and I'm still in college," I offered.

She shook her head. "A lot of people are," she replied, still not satisfied.

God knows you are asking for it, lady, I thought, God knows, because I could hit you with some shit that would knock your butt into next week. I was frustrated, she wanted me to be, and then all of a sudden it flew out into the air before I could catch it, it just flew out—

"I HAVE A MOUTH LIKE A SAILOR."

She didn't nod, or smile, or say anything. She went for her laptop and began typing furiously.

I did not get the job.

My friends Colleen and Jeff thought of a brilliant business venture that I can be included in. It's the Anti-Christ of Glamour Shots, that place that gets you all dolled up like Barbara

Mandrell and then takes your picture. We want to call our place "Hip N' Hot," and what we would do is make people over with the use black hair dye, give them dreadlocks, nose rings, neck tattoos, shaved eyebrows, and, when required, dental implants. We would also allow partial nudity.

For the rest of my life I guess I could hang out at my grandparents, which is always fun. Especially when Pop Pop gets mad at Nana and pretends to have Tourette's Syndrome, and he starts twitching all over violently and shouts out "Bitch! BEEP! Bitch!" Nana usually just looks over at him, shakes her head and says, "For Christ's sake, shut up, Nick. I'm watching my program."

The only problem with hanging out over there is that Pop Pop tries to use me to get famous, like when he said, "I'll pay you fifty dollars if you write a nice little column called 'What My Pop Pop Means To Me,'" or "Why don't you write about that time when I was in the hospital and I had my stomach removed and that son of a bitch orderly tried to kill me by giving me the wrong pills? That's funny. I think people would laugh." If it sounds like he's starved for attention, he's not, he just refuses to get a hearing aid so he misses out on a lot of stuff and what he does hear always gets all messed up anyway. Like the other day, he asked he, "Did you hear? That girl is suing her husband -- Michael Jackson's sister -- what's her name? Tanya? Toyota?"

My friend Bernie suggested that I join the Peace Corps, but I don't know. I have this vision of myself sitting on some frozen mountain in a goatskin coat, the only person within a 300-mile radius that has any semblance to teeth, digging through the mud with a stick to gather enough worms to feed an entire village for dinner. I'm not a 'people person,' actually I hate people, and the one ounce of patience God gave me when I was born got used up a long time ago.

My friend Stacy suggested that I open an optical boutique called "4 Ize 4 U," because I was an optician a ways back, if you can believe that. I don't think this is a good idea, because I do believe that while I was employed as a health care worker, I seriously maimed people. I fit one old lady with those invisible bifocals so badly that she fell down a flight of stairs a couple of days later and got a black eye. I told her she needed to 'adjust to them,' because I didn't know what else to do, and the next week she got into a car accident and tore off the left side of her car because she didn't see a truck that was hauling grapefruits. She came back and cried at the counter. Sobbed like a baby. I told her she wasn't trying hard enough and she had to give these things time.

I could also take the few remaining years of my life in bed, smoking and drinking whiskey from the bottle, trying to unconfuse myself about fish, fire and dog bands, like School of Fish, Fishbone, Phish, Jellyfish, firehose, Firehouse, Temple of the Dog, Dog Society, Crime Dog until I finally drive myself more insane than I already am and then fall asleep and catch my bed on fire with a smoldering cigarette.

When I asked Troy what I should do after graduation, he just said, "Drink."

Another option I have is to join my ex-boyfriend, a former mohawked punk who now specializes in believing in fairies and having out-of-body experiences. I suppose I could dedicate my life to sharing everything I don't have with everyone else who doesn't have anything, selling rice burritos at Grateful Dead concerts, weaving yarn into people's hair and trying to figure out what kind of mood Jerry is in simply by what he was wearing. "He's wearing black, man. Something's wrong." Nothing's wrong, goddammit. The asshole is selling ties for 75 bucks a pop, I'd be pretty damn happy about that. I couldn't make that much money at a garage sale or if I sold my heart to medical science.

I'm out of here, this is it. I no longer have a job, I have no reason to get out of bed in the morning and I am not a good listener.

But I know this: IF I eat a sandwich with onions on it before my next job interview. I shall not be so courteous, I shall not be so thoughtful and I will pretend to listen to every word the interviewer has said.

Survival of the Fittest— Well, Kind Of

I had high hopes for the May morning after my Make-Believe Graduation. I cleared all the food and crumbs out of my bed the night before, tucked the blankets in securely, placed a pack of smokes, a lighter and a Pepsi on my night table and tacked two black sheets over the bedroom window so that the sun couldn't sneak in before I was ready to get up at three.

I forgot one thing.

It seemed, as soon as I got home and sunk my head into my pillow and my eyes rolled back in my head, something shrieked in my ear. And that demon from Hell was the phone.

Impossible, I immediately thought, as my brain sourly attempted to flicker on, *impossible,* no one I know is functioning well enough at this point in the night to *remember* a phone number, let alone *dial* it. No one would dare to denounce the sanctity of the Two O' Clock Rule, which used to be the Twelve O'clock Rule until 75% of my friends decided to become unemployed and we voted to have the rule amended to two o'clock. The Two O'clock Rule states, more or less in its entirety, that it is "against Holy

Nocturnal Law to purposefully and intentionally disrupt and shatter the sleeping patterns to those who condemn and shun daylight, especially when those persons are inebriates, with the use of a phone call or social visit. Doing so may kill those comatose with loud sound vibrations and as will the exertion of speaking." The only exception to this rule that we could think of for making a phone call before this appointed time concerned the efforts of a troubled friend trying making bail.

There is no one I associate myself with that would execute a phone call so repulsive in its conception, no one I know that yearns to communicate with me while I am hung and woken suddenly because when I am, I'm nastier than when I'm drunk. There is no one, no enemy, no ex-boyfriend, and no creditor that will dare to experience that, especially before I have my first three cigarettes and go to the bathroom. There is no sane person in this world that would, no person except My Mother.

Before I even screamed "WHAT?" into the receiver, I heard her say, "For Christ's sake, don't tell me you're still sleeping! I've been up for eight hours!"

"You're killing me, Mom."

"Did you find a job yet?"

"I'm almost dead, Mom," I said, wondering if My Mother had swarmed on my sister, who had also graduated the day before.

Then I suddenly remembered that, unlike myself, my sister possessed qualities of responsibility, ambition and survival instincts, whereas my survival instincts consisted solely of lighting an entire pack of cigarettes end to end because I only had one match.

"Have you applied anywhere? How are you going to support yourself? Your sister already has three interviews. Your father and I aren't going to support you forever."

Okay, so I had been living on the dole while I was in college, collecting my allowance of $70 a week from their house every Thursday, which is when I would also steal food, because 70 bucks does not stretch far. And every Thursday, My Mother would hand over the three 20's and a ten all folded together tightly, and proclaim as it touched my fingertips, "And *don't* spend this at the bar buying drinks for all your friends."

My mother was convinced I was living as glamorously as Heidi Fleiss. "What do you do with that money?" she asked me one Thursday when she caught me stuffing my father's Oreos into my purse.

I ran down the list. "Twenty dollars for gas, seventeen for a carton of cigarettes and twenty dollars for dog and cat food," I answered. "And that leaves me thirteen dollars to live on."

"Well, if you didn't spend all of that money on gas so you could drive to bars and on cigarettes, you might have enough money to buy your own food," she said. *"Put the Oreos back."*

I lived through this summer on the dole, trying to find a job after three o'clock during the days and trying to find drink specials at night that would stretch my thirteen dollars of mad money from Thursday to Thursday. These were the Salad Days.

I didn't find a job until the end of August, and when I told my mother I had an interview, I heard the tears of elation swelling down on her cheeks, drowning her cigarette. "Thank God," she wept, "Thank God. You have an interview for a full-time job. *It is full-time, isn't it?*"

"Yes, Mom."

"We are so proud of you. Your sister has an interview, too."

I went to the interview with my resume in hand, and I even wore a dress and panty hose with the crotch still intact. I sat on the couch in the reception area, and was euphoric to find an ashtray on the front desk, full of smashed butts. This is a great and holy place, I thought. People smoke here. My kind of people.

My new potential boss walked through the door, and a familiar face was he, though I couldn't place him right away. We started the interview and I noticed he was looking at me strangely like he knew me, too, and I looked back and then it hit me, though not all at once:

Fourth of July, 1993; I am very drunk. I am going to my friend Kate's house for a barbeque, I slam the front door open, exclaiming, "I want to set something on fire!" and throw all 15 pounds of my purse down, next to a long-haired man sitting cross-legged on the floor. It lands with a solid THUD, and he starts rummaging through it, and exclaims, "Look at all of this shit! You've got a fifth of Jack Daniel's in here!" and begins to throw what he thinks to be insignificant empty cigarette packs, little scraps of paper and gum wrappers away. I am immediately offended and frightened that he may want some of the bottle, so I scream, kicking him as hard as I could in the leg, *"Who the hell are you, little man?"*

And that little man is the same little man sitting across from me now.

He looks at me quizzically. "Do you know Kate?" he asks.

"I DON'T KNOW ANY KATE," I blurt out.

"Didn't I clean out your purse and you--"

Oh shit. This is the part of your life, Laurie, when your past comes back to haunt you, remember? Your Mother told you this would happen. You always thought it would take the form of kinky photographs, but you never wanted to be Miss America anyway.

You'll never get off the dole and $70 Thursdays. Never never never. You'll never get a job where you can smoke at your desk, you loser. Just confess.

"YES I WAS THE ONE WHO KICKED YOU AND CALLED YOU LITTLE MAN. BUT I WAS DRUNK. IT WAS A HOLIDAY. IT REALLY WAS."

And I got the job.

I am a receptionist.

I work every day.

I make the coffee for the Little Man.

I make more, though not much more, than $70 a week.

My sister also got a job, and she came over to tell me the news. She makes $70 in a day.

"I got the job!" she cried.

"So did I!" I cried back.

"I have my own office!" she said.

"I have a swivel chair!" I said back.

"I have my own phone extension!" she exclaimed.

"I learned how to put toner in the copier!" I exclaimed back.

"I have my own business cards!" she shouted.

I smiled. She may have had the cards, she may have had the voice mail, but there was one thing left: there was no way she had the prime perk that I did.

"Who gives a rat's ass?" I shouted back, about to win embrace victory. "I can smoke at my desk!"

And that's what I call survival instinct.

Smoking Eyeballs, A Mug Full of Urine and Why Little Man Shakes His Head

I kinda like my job.

I've been there for three weeks now, and I get in trouble almost every day. The first reason I get in trouble is because I have a boss, Little Man. I'm not used to having bosses, in fact, I'm used to being the boss and bossing other people around, because I am bossy by nature. I can't help this. I'm a Scorpio and I'm from New York.

The first time Little Man got mad at me was when a client invited our office to some bowling party, and they paid for the food, the hooch, the bowling and they also gave us presents.

By the time my tribe arrived, the free booze tab had evaporated and the once-beautiful free buffet was reduced to a slab of dried bologna and a bowl of salsa. I was starving, hadn't eaten a thing all day, so I took the bologna, dipped it in the salsa and headed for the bar.

While I was waiting for my drink, I noticed that the host, nicely groomed and sporting smart slacks, was passing out free CDs to the people I worked with, so I ran over to get my share and sure enough, he handed me a full bag of them. Which meant I could pay my phone bill.

I was bored by the bowling part of the party, but there is a certain atmosphere that breeds in a bowling alley that makes you need to drink. It's the sweat, it's the aroma of stale nachos, and it's the yellow armpit stains of the patrons. It's the exhilaration of putting your feet into a place where a million faceless feet have perspired before. It's the bleary, worn-out look in their eyes. I was in a bowling alley, dammitt! I must drink! And I did. I drank a lot. It got to the point that the bartender would pour a drink every fifteen minutes and I would just swing by, pick it up and drop her $2.50.

Needless to say, Hurricane Bitter Drunk was conceived, gestated in a number of hours and then born of an empty stomach and sour mash whiskey. I spotted our host, felt the greed bloat in my veins and motioned him over to our alley. "Hey Mister Free CDs!" I growled, "Come here!"

With a jaunty look on his face, he hopped over to us and spirited, "Hey gals! How's everything going? Are you having fun?"

Holding my glass of belligerence in one hand and a cigarette in the other, I sauntered towards him, actually staggered, and barked, "You got any more CDs to give me?"

"No, I sure don't," he said as his jolly expression turned to pure white fear and his voice trembled and he started to back away from me. "I'm afraid they're all gone."

I would have none of that.

"Don't be stingy with me, Music Man!" I shrieked, pointing at him with my smoking hand. "I've got kids to feed!"

He did not think this was funny. But I did, and figured that a night isn't worth stink on shit if you haven't alienated and frightened at least one person. I thought it was hilarious until I woke up in the morning and remembered what I said to our gracious host in the nice slacks and how amazingly pliable those slacks were when he hurdled the bowling ball wall to get away from me.

The next day, Little Man came up to my desk after someone snitched on me, and he was shaking his head.

"Laurie Laurie Laurie," he said, putting both hands on my desk. "When someone pays for the company to eat free, to drink free and to bowl free, it isn't generally a good idea to verbally assault them before the night is over."

I only had one defense.

"I paid for my own drinks," I offered.

From now on, I'm not allowed to go to work-related functions and drink anything but pure Pepsi, whether I pay for it or not.

I also got in trouble because, since I am the receptionist, I have full access to the intercom system and I have to page people when they get phone calls. This means, essentially, that I have a captive audience of 30 people in a warehouse that I can terrorize and bully whenever I feel like it, all at my fingertips. It's like having my own radio show.

"John White, the girl your brought home is on line one and would like to know why there is bacon in your fridge when you told her you were a vegan. John White, line one."

"John Myers, your ex-girlfriend is on line two and she said the DNA test results just came in and now you owe her money every month. John Myers, line two."

"Barry Gibson, your connection is on line two and will be waiting outside in the parking lot after work for the $200 you still owe him. He will be the one with the crowbar, he said. Barry Gibson, line two."

"Rory Watkins, your parole officer is on line three and said you'd better get your bracelet back on and mow that church lawn. Rory Watkins, line three."

I was having a ton of fun with my show until Little Man shook his head and told me to *Knock It Off* because I was "distracting the boys in the warehouse. You already have 10 of them filing sexual harassment charges against you," he warned.

Another part of my job is giving all the newly hired people their tax forms to fill out. It took me a couple of days to discover what joy this task could bring. So, one Friday I decided to see how much fun I could have with a new hire.

"Um, how much did they tell you about this job?" I asked him.

"Not much," he said as he laughed a little.

"Let me give you a tip, okay?" I said, leaning forward. He nodded. "Whenever you're back there, working with the gasoline and paint thinner, it isn't a good idea to smoke."

"Oh, I don't smoke," he said, shaking his head, "I don't smoke."

"Well, that's good," I offered, "Because the guy who had the job before you, Squeaks, he did smoke, and he kind of—got singed. Exploded, really. God, it was a mess, I don't like to talk about it, his eyes were just hanging there, smoking, and that smell--"

"No, no, don't smoke," he assured me in a shaky voice. "Never did, don't smoke."

"Ever smelled charred flesh?"

"Uh-uh."

I shook my head. "Can't get it out of my nostrils," I said. "And it's been *four* days. Gruesome. If there's any chemicals kind of spilled anywhere and you see someone about to light up, you just run like hell."

I smiled. "Are you done with that?" I asked, pointing to the tax forms. He nodded.

"Okay," I said, handing him my half-full coffee cup. "Take this into the bathroom, dump that old coffee out. I need a urine sample, so fill it to the top, please."

"You're kidding."

"No, I'm not. We drug test now."

"Well, this isn't very sanitary," he protested.

"Well, it's the best I can do right this minute," I sighed. "I'll be along in a second to slide a paper plate under the door. I need a fecal sample as well. We're all out of baggies."

When Little Man found out about it, he shook his head a lot, and then said sternly, "Quit spooking the new people! You must stop!"

"Okay, boss," I said meekly, "I will stop spooking the new people," all the while spying the 75-gallon fish tank that promised endless hours of entertainment.

Nobody Likes a Quitter

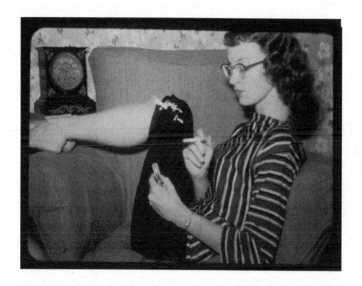

The cigarette pack weighed as much as if there was nothing in it.

I shook it. All I heard where the tumble of tobacco flakes being tossed from one side of the pack to the other.

I could have sworn I had one left.

I gave up on shaking it and ripped it open instead.

I was *sure* I had one left. I wouldn't have smoked that last one in such a hurry if I knew it was going to be my last.

Looking down at the shredded paper and cellophane in my hands, I realized that I should have enjoyed my last cigarette a little bit more.

I was out. Completely, 100%, out of cigarettes, and I was right smack in the middle of nicotine fit.

It was 115 degrees outside.

My car was in the shop with a seriously busted axle.

The closest store was a half-mile away.

I threw my head into my hands and cursed myself for not buying a house next door to a Circle K.

Either way, through nicotine withdrawal or a perilous pedestrian journey through the desert, I was going to be taking a Death Trip very, very soon.

I was afraid.

All of a sudden, I thought of something incredibly stupid. It was so stupid, I even laughed out loud at it.

I should quit. Now is the perfect time to quit. I'm out of cigarettes, which is amazing because I usually buy two cartons at a time. I need to use an inhaler to breathe if I want to go to sleep. My throat always hurts. I smell. My fingers are yellow. My breath is bad. I can't laugh without coughing up what looks like an embryo.

And, SOMEHOW, *somehow,* that argument worked. It made *sense.* I honestly don't know what happened to me, but I decided that I was going to quit.

It was 2:13 p.m. on Tuesday, August 1. I remember hearing somewhere than the urge to smoke a cigarette will pass in 10 minutes whether you have one or not.

At 2:24 p.m. on Tuesday, August 1 I knew it was the biggest, cruelest lie anyone had ever told.

By the time my husband came home, I had only a pinkie's grasp left on my sanity. I had locked the cat, the dog and myself in separate bedrooms so they wouldn't agitate me into killing them and I hid under the covers in my bed.

I decided I wasn't going to tell him about my lifestyle change until he noticed, just to see how attentive he was. When I heard the front door shut, I rocketed myself out of bed and decided to fix dinner.

"Hi, honey," I said as I met in coming down the hall. "What would you like for dinner?"

"Oh, anything is fine," he answered.

This made me mad. It made me furious.

"Why can't you," I said, immediately throwing my hands on my hips, "Just this once, *make a decision? Huh?* Why is it always MY job, Mr. Anything's Fine? Grow a backbone, for Christ's sake! WHY IS THIS WHOLE HOUSE MY RESPONSIBILITY?"

"Okay," my husband said as he took a deep breath. "How about chicken?"

So I made some Hamburger Helper, calmed myself down a bit, put dinner on the table. We turned on the TV, sat down and he reached for my plate, scooped a bunch of green beans, Hamburger Helper and potatoes onto it, then sat it back down in front of me.

"What did you do that for?' I asked.

"I just did it to be nice," he replied.

"I can get my own food!" I yelled. "I don't like it when it touches!"

"Did your mom come over today?" he said, putting his hand on my shoulder.

"AHHHH!" I shouted. "Don't touch me! Don't touch me when I'm eating!"

"What the hell is wrong with you?" he pleaded.

"I quit smoking today!" I cried. "I haven't had a cigarette in almost four hours. Right now, I would stick my tongue up your nose if I could smoke afterwards."

But I couldn't smoke. I had made the decision not to. When the desire to light up hit me, which it did every two minutes, I just told myself over and over again that smoking wasn't an option. I began "smoking" pens, pencils, straws, old butts and rolled-up pieces of paper. I ate sunflower seeds (which didn't help) and swallowed bottles of Golden Seal (which made me *very* regular).

It occurred to me when I had survived day two, after I had verbally assaulted a clerk at a book store written a nasty, obscene letter to the editor and hadn't slept in 30 hours that smoking affected a larger chunk of my life than I had originally thought, like *the whole thing*. Smoking was a bigger hobby than I had previously thought, which made sense. It was my *only* hobby.

The urge to smoke, the desire, the craving, the need — it wasn't any such thing; it was so far beyond that. It had become an **emotion**. In fact, my thought process no longer even *had* a word for smoking. When my body wanted to do it, it just sent out a quick firing synapses thing that overwhelmed and smothered my whole person with the command and the feeling that I was about to burst out uncontrollably into tears. It didn't tell me to smoke. Instead, it said, "DO THAT THING."

Every time the phone rings and it's for me.

DO THAT THING.

When take the last bite of any meal.

DO THAT THING.

If I get a new magazine or book and I want to read it on the potty.

DO THAT THING.

When it's normally time for my morning business.

DO THAT THING.

When I wake up.
DO THAT THING.
When I sit down in front of a keyboard.
DO THAT THING NOW.

Nothing was fun anymore. Well, nothing except for one thing, and even that came to a screeching halt.

We were at Costco the following Saturday, shopping for pickles, pretzels, car window shades and 409. I suddenly realized how late in the afternoon it was, and rushed him over to the snack part of Price Club where they give out samples, since the free food party is generally over after lunchtime.

I was having a lucky day, gathering up two samples each of peach pie, stuffed pork roast, ravioli in pesto sauce and morning fruit bars, one for me and one for mi esposo. Luckily, he wasn't hungry, so I got to have two of *everything*, and I was happy as a shithouse rat, especially when I captured the chocolate chip cookie samples. I was about to load a cookie chaser into my mouth when he grabbed my arm and herded me over into a quiet, unoccupied corner.

"Laurie, I didn't want to mention this here," he began with a very serious look on his face, "But you haven't stopped chewing since Tuesday. In two weeks, you're going to ask me how you got so fat, and I'm afraid I'm going to have to tell you. So, to avoid all of that, I'm asking you now to spit out that cookie."

"But it's a *chocolate* cookie," I mumbled with my mouth full. "It's a *good* chocolate cookie. It's moist and chewy."

He held out his hand.

I spit back into the paper cup.

"You don't understand," I complained. "Nothing can make me happy unless I can inhale it."

"But you're a non-smoker now," he informed me. "You're going to have to find something to replace cigarettes."

"Then give me back that damn replacement cookie," I insisted. "And you are wrong, dead wrong. I am *not* a non-smoker. I am still a smoker, but one that isn't allowed to smoke!"

"I'm telling you that you need a hobby," he reiterated. "Macramé, porcelain plate collecting? Yoga? What about kick boxing?"

"I'm going to quit," I decided.

"You already did," he replied.

"I'm *quitting* quitting smoking," I clarified.

"Okay, then take a deep breath," he instructed.

I did.

"What did you hear?" he asked. I shook my head.

"Exactly. If you had smoked regularly today, your lungs would have screamed like a rape whistle," my husband mentioned.

He was right. I went back to quitting in the singular, and discovered a new hobby. Withdrawal.

After all, I figured, nobody likes a quitter.

Especially a two-faced one.

I Am Adult

The Ryder truck wasn't ready.

In fact, no trucks were available at the outfit where I had made the reservation, which turned out to be a simply plywood counter, a phone and a chair that was located inside an ammunition and arms shop that specialized in stun guns, tasers and numchucks.

I was moving. Again. Three months after I had hauled every possession that was my life to our new house, I had been offered a job as an editor with a new magazine in Tucson.

I couldn't turn it down; in my eyes, it was the opportunity of a lifetime, a dream job come true. My last job had been a bona fide disaster, working for an heiress in a job description that changed every week (writing, public relations, fund raising, teen advisor, babysitter, maid and actor) for a company that really only existed inside my boss' head. I had watched 40 of my friends as they were laid-off due to "financial difficulties," one by one or in groups, while she easily slammed down $3,000 for a ceramic fairy sitting on a log or $2,500 for an equally insipid framed lighthouse constructed entirely of flat toothpicks. She had a habit of firing people right before they received their vacation or while they were actually on it, and my anniversary was days away. So I took the Tucson job, got laid off a year and a day after I began working for the heiress (a bitter miscalculation on her part) found a funky, downtown apartment, bought a new car and was ready to become a commuter.

I didn't really understand the implications until my sister mentioned that since I would be driving back and forth from Phoenix to Tucson, from Tucson to Phoenix, I should get a cellular phone. I balked, laughed out loud, and then became quiet. This could only mean one thing: if I was commuting someplace, if I was commuting to anything, if I needed a cellular phone, I had become an adult.

Commuters aren't kids, they're grown-ups.

Okay, so I had gotten married, become a Costco member, bought a house, watched a nephew being born and watched my grandfather as he died. Pretty big and some awful stuff, but mainly nothing that it takes an astounding maturity level to do.

Still, I hadn't picked up on the clues. I thought that as long as I was still eating Froot Loops for dinner, forgot to brush my teeth on occasion and didn't return things I borrowed from other people, I'd be okay, I was safe. I wasn't even close to thinking about an IRA, 401K and still don't know what a portfolio is.

But I wasn't safe. In fact, times were terribly dangerous.

When did this happen, I asked myself, as my mind raced. How could this change have taken place and I didn't see the warning signs? And there were so many. I started thinking.

About a year ago, I ordered a book by mail.

Last February, I saw a pair of Rockport sandals at Costco and thought, those are cute, they'd be comfortable. . . and I could wear them with socks.

I got approved for a Visa, and the bad things on my credit history were expiring with the statute of limitations.

I had curtains on my windows, not sheets.

I got a catalog from Pottery Barn.

And then I realized the event that confirmed it, that solidified my passage into adulthood with no turning back, no second chances, no reprieve.

I got my emissions test done and paid my car registration. . . ON TIME. No late fees. No tickets. No explaining to the judge why I was so irresponsible and flaky.

Was that really me?

It looked like it. It's true. I am an adult.

So when the Ryder truck lady explained to me that their fleet of trucks had simply vanished overnight and that I was going to have to find another rental truck on a Saturday afternoon, I remembered I was an adult, composed myself and only used the "F" word twice.

I remembered I was an adult after we had hauled my stuff 100 miles to Tucson in 95-degree heat, unloaded it and watched my husband drive back to Phoenix without me. I remembered I was an adult as I unpacked my stuff alone, feeling as scared and anxious as a kid who had just gone away to college. And I remember I am an adult every Friday afternoon when toss my cellular phone into my purse, throw my bag of dirty laundry into my back seat and get on the highway to drive 100 miles back to my house, my husband, my dog and my nephew.

And when the office manager at the magazine office in Tucson gave me my orientation, she went over vacations, sick leave, health insurance and tax forms.

"There's one more thing," she said, after I thought she was finished. "You're eligible for the 401K and profit sharing plans. Interested?"

After what seemed like a long while, I smiled, laughed inside myself.
I nodded.

It's A Hit!

By the time I saw the couple running in the crosswalk, it was already too late. I was three-quarters of the way through a left hand turn, and although the pedestrians were really in no danger of being kissed by my car, I responded to their exaggerated and flagrant and nearly Broadway-caliber jump back with a faux wince and a wave to as I finished the turn.

But apparently, they weren't the only ones who presumed that the sands in their mortal hourglass had nearly stopped short, because as soon as I finished that turn, lights flashed in my rearview mirror. I didn't protest, argue or debate the officer as he wrote out the ticket that I really didn't deserve. I wasn't going to say anything, mainly because that ticket had been chasing me for almost a decade and just now had caught up.

It was a July about nine years ago, and I was working at a tiny little magazine my friends and I had started. Our "office" was in a former motel — the rent was cheap, and more frequently than not, the air conditioner was nothing but a faint memory. On those unfortunate occasions, when it was 118 outside, it was 118 inside, too.

It was one of those miserable air conditioner-less days in which if you sat still long enough without a drink of water, you could watch yourself begin to mummify. Someone mentioned sno cones, and I volunteered immediately because I had air conditioning in my car and I had sweated so much over my keyboard that the keys were sticking. Off I went around the corner with the sno cone order in my hand, I had just turned the steering wheel and was making sure traffic was clear when I heard an odd noise, as if someone had thrown a rather large potato at my car, and when I looked up, there was a man. On the other side of my windshield, his head parallel to my head, his hands on the glass on either side of his face.

There was a man.

His mouth wide open, his eyeballs took on the size of hard-boiled eggs, and he was just lying on my car, all over the hood. It was like I was at an aquarium, and all of a sudden, there was a merman. He stayed there for a second, and when I stopped the car, he rolled backwards, his hands squeaking against the hood of my car, and then he fell off.

"What a nutjob! Are you crazy?" I actually cried out loud, and I looked past the man, now burning his exposed skin on the pavement, and saw a bike on the ground, the wheels still spinning.

"Why are you jumping on my car if you already have a ride? You scared me half to death!" I continued, and then I understood as people from all over began to gather around him and help him up.

Then it hit me.

Holy shit.

I just hit him.

Holy shit. HOLY SHIT! *I just hit a guy.* I just hit THAT GUY that rolled off my car like a giant Hickory Farms summer sausage. Where did he come from? How did this happen? I didn't even see him! Am I sure that I hit him? Maybe he really did just jump on my car! I can't believe this! Did this really happen or is he a bad heat mirage?

I didn't know what to do, so I sat there for a moment, just in shock, and then shut off the car.

"Oh, shit!" I yelled as I ran over to him. "Are you okay? *Are you okay!*"

With the help of some passersby, the man stood up and dusted himself off, then picked up his still-spinning bike up off of the street and the cowboy hat I had apparently knocked right off his head. I felt horrible. But not horrible enough to give him my insurance card without feeling out the situation first.

"Are you okay?" I asked the man again. "I didn't even see you until we were eye to eye when you landed on my car! I thought I'm so sorry! I really am sorry! Can I help you, are you hurt?"

"I okay," he said with a nod. "I okay." Then he pointed to the bike. "Okay. Okay. I okay."

"Really? Are you sure? Do you want me to call someone, an ambulance?" I insisted.

The man kept shaking his head and held onto the bike.

"What we really should do is call the police," a nosy bystander who had been waiting for the bus said.

Before I could step forward and say, "Um, excuse me, this is OUR accident, *his and mine,* and we don't really need any input from you, *bus person*, you don't even drive a car, so what would you know about hitting somebody, *anyway?*", my victim started shaking his hand and became visibly alarmed.

"No, no, no, no police," he repeated, "No police! I okay, I okay, I okay!"

Clearly, the man had issues with the police, and frankly, I was no fool, I didn't want the police poking around either. I mean, not only was I looking at a rate hike in my insurance for tossing a bicyclist, but also there may have even been potential for something as unthinkable as jail time or even driving school.

"We should call the police," the bus person declared again, which was enough to send my victim into something of a meltdown.

"Por favor, por favor, no police," he begged. "No police!"

"Are you not a citizen?" I said to him quietly through clenched teeth, but he looked at me as if he had no idea what I was saying. "Illegal? Are you illegal?"

And to that, I might as well have just flashed him a badge that said INS, because that man, despite the fact that he had just been hit, albeit lightly — it would really be more concise to say he was simply tapped — by a car, got on his piece-of-shit, broken, dented and mangled bike and sped away like he was Lance Armstrong.

"Good job," I said to the bus person as I nodded at her. "That was a good move. I was just about to get him a sno cone!"

Ever since, I have felt terrible about hitting that illegal alien on a bike, but if I may be honest, if you're going to smack someone with your car on the way to get a sno cone, it's sadly preferable to have one who's about an arm's length on the other side of the law. Especially when his punishment would have been way worse than mine should the authorities been on scene. I'd gladly take jail time and spend my days picking up trash in an orange jumpsuit on the side of the road over living in Mexico, which the parts I've been in makes Indian reservations look like Hilton Head in comparison. At least in jail I'd have air conditioning and basic cable and I probably wouldn't have to eat my pet.

So when I saw the flashing lights behind me, I had everything in place and handed it over to the officer, did not beg for a warning, and I gladly accepted a ticket for NOT hitting those people in the crosswalk in lieu of the one that had already landed on the hood of my car like he was a part from the space shuttle.

"Be a little careful about those crosswalks," the cop reminded me. "You can turn after the pedestrians have passed you, but don't turn in front of them."

"I can tell you I'll be very, very careful," I said.

"And make sure you watch out for bicyclists, they can pop out of nowhere," the cop told me.

I just smiled and handed over my insurance card.

Long-time Listener, First Time Caller

No first-time homeowner, no matter how savvy, insightful and clairvoyant, can ever prepare themselves for the anguish and tribulations that are enveloped in the mortgage loan process.

I've been more relaxed at the dentist's, even when he pulled a back molar out of my head with his bare hands; at job interviews when I called the new prospective boss by the wrong name; or when I'm an hour away from a heavy deadline and my computer crashes.

Having found our dream house, a Veteran's Administration-acquired 1926 blond brick bungalow near downtown, my husband and I thought we had hit three cherries in the slot machine of real estate. Although we weren't in the market for a VA house, the deal was too good to pass up; three bedrooms, wood floors, fireplace, and guest house on nearly a quarter of an acre stamp of land. Our realtor placed our bid and we waited for two weeks until the victor — the highest bidder — was announced

The night before, I spent the hours pacing back and forth from the bathroom, sicker than any flu bug had kicked me down. I remained in bed the next day, completely drained and unable to go to work, with the telephone beside me, resting on a pillow. Just before sundown, the call finally came, and our realtor told us we got the bid. The house was almost ours. I felt as if Ed McMahon had arrived at my door, bearing a six-foot long check, sirens and a camera crew, and, catching me in a towel, offered me a modeling contract.

The hard part was over, I thought, breathed a sigh of relief, and started collecting boxes for our anticipated move. A loan officer called and politely told us what documents we'd need to prepare for the loan application; tax forms, pay stubs, our marriage license, and anything else we deemed applicable. I rushed to Home Depot and began picking out paint colors.

That was the last day that I remember as a normal, functioning member of society. The phone started ringing with calls from the realtor, the increasingly less polite loan officer and insurance agents.

Why was I late on a payment for a microwave I had purchased at Montgomery Ward's in the spring of 1990?

Where were my college transcripts?

How much was my car and that microwave worth now?

What were the dimensions and sex of our pets?

Did we have the photocopies of our mattress tags that we weren't supposed to remove?

Why did I ask Mike Collins to the Sadie Hawkins dance in seventh grade? Didn't I know he would reject me? I'm not a very bright girl, am I?

Not only did we have to provide these things (and usually that same day they were requested, by 4 p.m. or the whole deal was off), I had to construct a letter of explanation for each and every one, in detail:

"I just remember chasing him all over school, crying, 'Why won't you go with me? Why?' He had passed me his extra SnoBall only the day before in fourth-period lunch."

I had received so many phone calls that I was starting to get in trouble at work. Even if I was working on something legitimate, my boss would pass my door and snidely remark, "Writing another letter of explanation, are we?"

I learned terms that I never wanted to know the meaning of—underwriting, principal accounts, trusts, and accrued interest—something I still don't understand. I had quit picking boxes out of dumpsters or holding up color chips to the light. The bank and VA people didn't care that my life was one big game to them—it was their job to destroy me, to whittle me down like the withered face of a shrunken head. We were experiencing the bitter ritual of Home Ownership Hazing, and I fully expected that before I was able to turn the key of the house in the lock if my front door, it would be jaggedly rubbed into the flesh of my chest.

I could imagine myself years from now, holed up in a room in boarding house with plywood windows, a bare light bulb sputtering and swinging above me. Swathed in a soiled bathrobe, I'd take a gulp from the bottle, wipe the liquor dribble from my mouth with the back of my hand and recount, "It all started with a bid. . ." as my front tooth fell to the floor on it's own. "Pick that up, would'ya, doll?"

When the day came four months later, we did get the keys to the house, we held them in our hands and wearily climbed up the steps of the porch. Although I had pictured this day the way it happens on real estate commercials, there were no balloons, no parade, and no flash of the camera. There was only the locksmith that VA suggested that we call, since "Everyone in the world has the keys to a VA house."

As the three of us walked inside to the living room with the coved ceilings, fireplace and wood floors, the locksmith turned to us briskly and remarked, "This is a VA house? Boy, you must have gotten this for a song."

My husband and I turned to each other, as if we were queued, and slowly began the chorus of "Never Enough," by The Cure.

Two Million Dollars, Clara the Fertile and the Alien Who Died of a Broken Heart

It was last night when I noticed it.

I was writing a research paper, had been at my computer for a couple of hours and I needed to take a break. It was one a.m., I needed to vomit up three more pages so I decided to smoke a cigarette. I walked around the house, trying to figure out if I should simply wipe my fat butt with the remainder of paper and just hand that in or if I could possibly stretch the last sentence I had in my head into ten more paragraphs.

I walked into the kitchen and turned on the light, which still amazes me because the bulb burned out two years ago and I used to have to carry a candle around in there until my ex-boyfriend graciously replaced the bulb last week. That is when I saw it.

It was Clara, or as I more commonly refer to her, The Evil. The Evil is one of my cats, the one I hate the most. She was eating out of a cat food bag that was on the counter, the contents of which were now splashed all over the floor in a flood of red jacks because she had gutted the bag with her eager claws and protruding fangs. But it wasn't the mess that caught my attention: it was her stomach. It was huge.

I was hoping it was a tumor or a big ball of cancer waiting to explode in her intestines, but unfortunately, I knew better. I knew that somewhere, buried beneath The Evil's leather demon skin were three, four, five, maybe six squirming Evil spawns, waiting to hatch and make my life a feline hell.

I already live in what my friends call The Barn, a house so overrun by animals that I had no choice but to relinquish every room but by bedroom to them. My bedroom is like a little studio apartment, with a bed, a TV, a VCR, a stereo, a computer, a table and chair so I can eat in there and everything else that I own that I don't want defecated on.

Big Max, a dog so fat that everyone thinks he's pregnant, is the king of the kitchen. His favorite spot is, of course, by his food bowl, and he lays next to it all day, waiting for me to fill it up with his food, which is called POOCH, except when I run out of food have to feed him whatever I have in the house like bread, Pop Tarts, pretzels and one time Oat Bran, which was a very bad idea.

Chelsea is Big Max's assistant dog, and she is intelligence deficient. She does whatever Big Max does. For instance, if she hears nature calling and wants to go out but he does not, she will remain indoors despite all prodding and dragging from me. Then, the minute I leave the room, she relieves herself on the floor. Her spot is under the coffee table in the living room.

Simon is my sister's cat that I am taking care of until she gets married, which is like three thousand years away or until she gets all of her Christmas pattern Lenox. If he dies before she walks down the aisle, I'm going to have him freeze dried and give him to her as a wedding gift for playing such a vicious trick on me. I have had this cat leap off of the floor and attach itself to my neck with the use of his claws, and there are 25 of them because he's a little deformed. He can also dial the phone and has learned how to change the message on my answering machine. Intellectually, he is gifted and had good paw-eye coordination. His favorite area is in the bathroom where he can shred 300 feet of toilet paper in five seconds flat, with those extra claws and all.

Barnaby is the favorite cat, and there's nothing wrong with him except that he's inbred and was born with half a tail so his balance isn't so good and sometimes he'll just tip over. He loves watching TV, especially the Montel Williams show.

The Evil, however, has plenty wrong with her. She is also inbred but exhibits extremely sociopathic behavior. I have never touched this cat, and I found her when she was three weeks old. This is why she was never spayed. I tried to pick her up once and she attacked me so heinously that my mother wanted to check me into Charter Hospital, a psych, rehab and eating disorder clinic that has franchises, like McDonalds, because she thought I slit my wrists. My mother is a walking commercial for Charter Hospital, anyway.

Every time she sees a flask in my purse or watches me pour A drink, she says, "I'm calling Charter Hospital because you need help!"

The last time I ate at my parents' house, we had wine for dinner because it was a special occasion since my Uncle Vinnie was visiting from New Jersey. My mother made macaroni, and my father was pouring the wine. When he asked if I wanted some, my mother grabbed the bottle out of his hands and screamed, "the last time she ate over here and got a hold of A BOTTLE, she finished it and started acting silly. I should have called Charter Hospital."

And this is partially true, because the time she was referring to was last Thanksgiving, you remember, when my family ate without me, which made me mad. After I had one glass of wine, my Pop Pop hid the bottle behind some fake flowers on the counter but I found it anyway. And then, to get back at them, I drank the whole thing myself. Now my family waits for me when we eat, and my Nana makes sure to tell me this. "See, Laurie?" she says. "We waited for you, so you don't write about us in your column anymore, okay?"

My friend Stacy once had this book called "A Book of Questions" which is supposed to craftily place you in moral dilemmas, and she was asking me stuff from it, like would eat a bowl of live bugs for $10,000 (no) or would you quit bathing and brushing your teeth for three months for $30,000 but you couldn't tell anybody why you were dirty (yes, I mostly do that anyway but for free).

Then she asked me, "Would you put your pet to death for $50,000?"

How could anyone, I thought, definitely "No." But then I got to thinking, I had five pets,

5 X $50,000 was *$250,000*, and I suddenly imagined myself in the garage with the car doors open, shouting, "Come on, everybody, we're going to the park!"

Two months ago, Clara disappeared. She was nowhere in the house, and I was so happy. I was using all of my psychic forces to keep her away, or to steer her to a house where she would be liked or wouldn't try to kill people. Colleen kept telling me, "She's going to come back, you know she will," but I stoutly denied it, "No, this time, I think she's really gone for good." Each day was a victory for me.

Well, Colleen, of course, was right. The Evil had been gone for a whole week when I heard her flinging herself against the side door, wanting to come in. I should have known better than to think she was gone forever, because she had done this once before when my friend Hoby was my houseguest and she hid in his room for three days, urinating on all of his clothes. At first I ignored the thumps, but then she started screaming when she hopped up on the window ledge and saw me inside.

I couldn't figure out how she got out of the house, though, until I saw a hole in the screen of the kitchen window that she had slashed to gain her freedom because her libido was evidently pulsating so stringently.

Then my mother called. I knew I had to tell her. I felt so dirty, like I was the one who had been tramping around with my panties off, servicing every male on the block, even though it was my cat that was an easy lay.

"Oh God," she said, and even though I couldn't see her, I knew she hand her hand on her head. "Oh God. Well, you should have expected it, because you're the one who let her escape. That's what happens. I told you a million times to get that damned thing spayed. What are you going to do now about your vacation if she has kittens?"

I forgot about my glorious vacation to Roswell, New Mexico, where a UFO crashed in 1947 and an alien survived and the Air Force and CIA took the alien and locked it up until it died a couple of years later of a broken heart. Now, there's a new UFO museum in Roswell with bits of the UFO on display. I was going to go there over Spring Break, and I wasn't going to miss it.

"It's not like La Maze, Mom," I said. "I don't think Clara needs a breathing coach or ice chips. She got herself into this mess, let her give birth by herself."

"What if there are complications?" my mother asked.

"Complications? What do you think, I might have to use a steak knife to perform a Caesarean on my cat?" I replied.

"You never know," my mother warned.

Of course I knew. If The Evil was going to have complications, it wouldn't be simple, like having the umbilical cord tied around a kitten's neck or anything like that. No, if she were going to have complications, it would be because she gave birth to Siamese twins, to two headed kittens, and there's nothing I can do about that. Not a damned thing until I get back from vacation.

I'm going to see that UFO if it kills me.

Brian Griffith, the Squirmin' Brain and Why I Had to Start Acting My Age

I have a good friend named BRIAN GRIFFITH who says that he doesn't read my column. He tells me that he glances at it every now and then just to scan it to see if he spots his name. I have a sneaky little suspicion that he doesn't read my column because is jealous that I sometimes use big words (more than four letters) and on occasion, I even know what they mean, and he's afraid that he might not. I wouldn't think that seeing his name in print would be all that thrilling for him, since he is in a BAND and should be used to it, being the quasi-semi-mega-Tempe-celebrity and that he his, according to him, much more better known than I. This is an entirely vital and substantial point of this column, so follow along with me throughout, please.

Anyway, one morning, BRIAN GRIFFITH left a message on my machine that I had to call him back immediately because there was an *EMERGENCY*.

I panicked, because BRIAN GRIFFITH (who once reportedly stated "Anyone can quit smoking; it takes a real man to face cancer") isn't an uptight person -- well, he is sort of Uptight OuttaSight; but he's not typically the anal-retentive sort -- he's typically anal-explosive; um, he cannot be termed as nervous -- okay, he's a walking, two-legged ulcer, but I panicked anyway.

So I called him, and when he answered, he told me that he forgot what the emergency was, but he had written it down on a piece of paper somewhere and he had to find it. When he had located the Emergency Scrap of Paper, he called me back and said:

"I want to wash your car for ten dollars, but I need the money up front."

"Up front? What are you talking about?" I replied.

"Inside and out. Ten dollars. Can you bring it over now?" BRIAN GRIFFITH asked.

I was still confused until he explained that he had lost his wallet the night before, paycheck and all, and that he was calling every single person on planet Earth that he knew to see if he could do odd jobs for them for money.

"And you want to clean my car?" I asked.

"Yes," BRIAN GRIFFITH said.

"Why don't you just go down to the frontage road next to the freeway with a borrowed child and pregnant woman and hold up a sign that says 'Hungry Family Will Work for Ten Dollars. Up Front'?"

"That's not respectable," he answered.

"And cleaning my car is?" I questioned.

There is something that I have to explain here. That something would be my car. It is a bigger version of my purse, yet smaller version of my house. It is the nucleus (that means "center," BRIAN GRIFFITH) of my existence, and contains vital pieces of my life, including, but not limited to: clothes, books, tapes, hats, toys, papers, renegade cigarette butts, shoes, bleach, food and drink.

I once found an article in some magazine that was supposed to determine your

personality by what items you carried around in your car, but it didn't work for me because I fit into every category they had, and there was eleven of them. Another time I took my car to the auto emissions
place, and the woman who worked there made me get out of the car because I wasn't doing something right so she had to do it. When she was in there, doing the revving thing or whatever it is they do, she asked my friend who was sitting in the passenger seat if I *lived* in my car, and then she got mad at me because she stuck her hand in the food pile between the seats and got Twinkie cream on her finger.

This is what comprises the flavor of my car, BRIAN GRIFFITH wanted to clean it, and he's even been *in* it. If offered, I wouldn't clean my own car for fifty thousand dollars, let alone ten.

My car has it's own scent that has never been captured anywhere else on earth, even in a laboratory under the foulest of conditions. My friend Colleen describes it as a "combination of stale Hostess products, cigarettes and cat food," while my friend Gene has commented that it smells like "bongwater" or "a car you would rent in Waco, Texas."

I have had three cars in the last ten years, and they all smelled the same, with the exception of the Sentra I had during the period of 1983-87, which occasionally expunged an aroma that can only be termed as a "meaty" smell. This happened when I spilled milk in the car and forgot to clean it up and then a carpet of mold grew underneath the floor mats on the passenger side. It was especially bad in the summertime. I didn't like that car very much because it had a small ashtray meant for baby smokers, and when it would get too full, butts would fly out when the windows were open and sometimes hit passengers in the face.

I also had a ghastly experience in that car which I will never forget. I was at school, and I needed to get something out of the trunk. I reached in, felt something wet and drew my hand back immediately. What was on my hand was thick and green and smelled like a bunch of monkeys. I knew I had to get whatever was in there *out*, and I reached in again, grabbed the wet thing and pulled it out and there, in my hand, in the school parking lot, was a plastic see-through bag with bubbling green spit in it. I held it up to the sun to look at it and that's when I saw The Squirmin' Brain, a round, fleshy ball the size of my fist that squiggled around in the bile (that means "the stuff you throw up during dry heaves," BRIAN GRIFFITH), and it had *things* hanging off of it. I entertained the thought of dumping it right there on the asphalt, but was afraid that the contents were noxious (that means "deadly," BRIAN GRIFFITH) and also that maybe that The Squirmin' Brain might scream.

The only thing that I can possibly think of is that The Squirmin' Brain had once been a head of lettuce, perhaps, that had rolled out of a grocery bag and just sort of fermented for a couple of months until I found it that morning.

Also in that car I unknowingly drove around for five days with a giant Queen-sized maxi pad stuck to my rear bumper because my wicked friend Monica thought it would be funny to put it there.

In this car that I have now I had a near-death experience, or one that would at least get me into some kind trouble just a couple of weeks ago. I was driving on the freeway with the windows open, and I was wearing one of my favorite hats. Hanging from the rear view mirror was a Killer Squid, like the kind that used to eat whole entire Navy ships in World War II, only my Killer Squid was smaller, made out of rubber and it squeaked when you poked it's belly.

The wind was whipping, and I was afraid that my hat would get blown off and then sucked out the other window, so I automatically reached up to grab it, only I did this, not with my free hand, but the one that carried the lit cigarette. The cigarette hit one of the writhing tentacles of the Killer Squid, decapitating the cherry, which went flying somewhere in the back of my car. I smelled the smoke but could

242

not figure out where it was coming from, so I was hitting everything that could possibly combust, (that means "burst into flames," BRIAN GRIFFITH) like paper, wrappers, and my hair.

I finally got to school and searched frantically for the smolder, (that means "the burning part," BRIAN GRIFFITH) but I still couldn't find it. I was already late, so I left the car in the lot and ran off to class, telling God that, since she knew how angry my father would be if I burnt my car down, I was hoping that she would try to take care of it.

After class, I asked people in the State Press newsroom if they had heard anything on the police radio about a car fire, and when they said no, I figured I was pretty safe. And I was. I checked my car twice, though, just in case.

Last week I was informed by my father that I needed to take my car in to get a tune-up, and that he was going to follow me to the garage and then give me a ride back. He was going to try to peek in my car, I knew it. I know my father, I know him well and I know that he bases my worth as a human being not by my personal and academic accomplishments, but on how clean the floorboards in my car are as well as the percentage of visibility through the tar-coated windows. He has threatened on numerous (that means "a lot," BRIAN GRIFFITH) occasions to take the car away if I didn't wash it on a regular basis, which I never did.

So I knew how pissed he'd be if he saw my car in it's regular state, I knew the lecture that would follow which is entitled "How Laurie Systematically Destroys Everything She Has Ever Been Given, Bought or Stolen So She'd Better Act Her Age And Dump That Goddamned Ashtray Out." So, with this cloud of ferocity brushing the top of my head, I decided that I had no other option but to tidy up my car.

It took five moving boxes to hold all the stuff I had carried around in the car, and that's not even messing with the trunk. I shook out the floor mats, cried as I emptied the ashtray, and even tried to pry all the pennies off the console which are cemented there by spilled, reduced and dried Pepsi syrup, though I eventually had to give up on that.

When my friends Troy and Bernie saw the car, they were speechless, mostly because they were drunk. Troy opened up the back door on the third try, smoothed his hand all over the upholstery of the seat because he had never seen it before, and purred, "Oh, may I sleep in this back seat for two nights only?"

Bernie was still silent, not very impressed, until he lunged for the ashtray, pulled it out and was not attacked by a Jack in the Box of lipstick-encrusted cigarette butts. He whirled (that means "a light-footed dance of sorts," BRIAN

GRIFFITH) around the street, his expression of amazement captured in dispersed segments by the shine of glowing street lamps, his hands on his head. "Maybe the Bible isn't a parable!" he proclaimed, exploding the 3 a.m. silence of the night. "Maybe Moses *did* part the Red Sea! It is the Dawning of the Age of Aquarius!"

What could I say?

I just laughed, thinking that I had saved ten dollars, my father just might recognize me now as a member of his own gene pool and that nothing, *nothing*, could ever get rid of that smell of bong water.

Thanks for the offer, BRIAN GRIFFITH. Next time, make it eight bucks and you've got yourself a deal, baby.

The Monkey Baby and Why My Kid Could Fix the Perfect Martini

My mother sometimes has an empty look in her eyes, a look as hollow as my soul and as desperate as a prostitute in Salt Lake City on a Sunday morning.

It's not a good thing. I know what she wants, I know what that look means. It happens every time she gets a birth announcement in the mail and it doesn't have her grandchild's name on it.

All of her other friends are grandmothers, she says, all of her other friends are on a first-name basis with the salespeople at Baby Gap and Imaginarium. All of her other friends have playpens set up in their living rooms, all of her other friends get to put up baby gates and get to work Fisher-Price walkie talkies.

"I want a Grandma's Brag Book," she cries.

She doesn't know what she's asking for, at least not from me. I just don't think I'm good mother material.

For example, my sidekick Nikki has a daughter, Ashlie. I call her "The Kid," and she's cool; she thinks Barney "sucks" and took hula dancing lessons.

On Halloween night at 6:30 p.m., Nikki and I were scrambling through the costume bins at Smitty's trying to piece together a Trick or Treating ensemble for The Kid because, like the Idiot Girls we are, we had waited until the last minute. (It's typical; on one road trip to Flagstaff this summer, our first stop in town had to be Payless Shoes because Nikki had forgotten to wear any. Individually, we are each tragedies; together, we are a disaster.)

There was nothing left in the bins, everything had been picked over so well that there were no ready-made costumes left besides fright wigs, red rubber noses and striped jumpsuits. You put a red rubber nose on an eight-year old and within a year, all the neighborhood cats will be missing.

I made some suggestions.

I found a little white, lacy flammable nightgown. I held it up. "Pregnant bride? All we'd need is a throw pillow."

"She's *four*, Laurie," Nikki answered. "She doesn't even know she has fallopian tubes yet."

I found a pair of baby fishnet stockings. "Child hooker? With a tube top and a hypodermic needle she'd have the best costume on the block," I hoped. "I've got my lipstick and my grandfather's a diabetic."

All I got was a dirty look.

"Here it is!" Nikki shouted, clutching a plastic package. "She's going to be a bunny." It was settled.

So we took the bunny package, which contained bunny ears, a white and pink bow tie and a really big cotton ball tail home to The Kid, and she was ecstatic. We threw The Kid's ballet clothes on her, a black leotard and black tights,

248

and I drew whiskers on her face with eyeliner. We stood back and looked.

"I'm a bunny! I'm a bunny!" Ashlie cried, jumping up and down.

"No, she's not," I whispered to Nikki. "Get her a tray and a Martini glass. Right on. She's a cocktail waitress."

Nikki gasped.

While Nikki searched in vain for a trick or treating bag, I pulled The Kid aside.

"You like Slurpees, don't you?" I asked her.

She nodded.

"Okay, then. I'll buy you the biggest Slurpee this town has ever seen if you do one thing. Do you want a Slurpee?"

Another nod.

"All right. When people ask you what you are, you say this. You say . . ."

It was agreed. Nikki came downstairs, bag in hand. "Are you ready?" she asked The Kid.

"Yes, Mommy," The Kid replied.

And we were off. Up and down the streets, we went house to house while The Kid knocked on doors and Nikki and I did just what my mom did when she used to take me trick or treating, which is stand on the curb and smoke, waiting for us to get tired.

It took eleven houses for someone to be interested enough in Halloween to do something besides throw a handful of Boston baked beans into The Kid's bag. The lady was an older woman, probably lived alone with her bottled-up loneliness and despair, you could tell because she wanted to talk and she was rambling.

"Aren't you adorable?" she cooed at The Kid.

"Yes," The Kid cooed back.

"Are you having fun?" the lady said, smiling and thinking that The Kid was just the cutest thing. "And what are you supposed to be?"

The Kid looked back at me and I nodded.

"I'm Gloria Steinem," The Kid replied with a grin, delivered perfectly, right on cue, I couldn't have done it better myself.

The lady immediately stood up, looked at Nikki and me as I ground out a cigarette butt on her curb, and quickly shut the door. I started to laugh.

The Kid was laughing, too, as she ran over to us.

"You're silly," she said, poking me in the arm.

"Yes, I am," I agreed, "But when you grow up, they call it 'manic depression.'"

You see, the thing is, if The Kid were my kid, she *would have* carried a tray and a Martini glass. My kid would know all kinds of things that other kids wouldn't, like where the smoking sections were in every mall, airport or Food

Stamp office. My kid would know how to not to let Mommy sleep on her back and how to roll her over on her side after happy hour. My kid would know that you stir gin and not shake it because it bruises so easily. My kid would know exactly what to do when I sent them to Circle K with a note that says "Marlboro Reds in a box." My kid would know never to ask, "Is he our new uncle?" in front of an overnight guest.

So it's probably not a good idea, in the state's opinion or mine that I reproduce. I figure that if I ever need to experience the joys of parenting so badly, I could just get a monkey. They don't need babysitters, they never learn to speak and they eat bugs from their own body.

I'm ever so content to be "Crazy/Drunk Aunt Laurie" who is never permitted to baby-sit, who is told, "My mom said I'm not allowed to eat anything at your house," and who leaves bloody red lips on cheeks when she gives kisses.

And I'm sorry, Mom. You've got two other daughters, one who is about to be married. Look their way with those haunting Gerber eyes when you pass your friends pushing strollers in Target. There's no way I can quit smoking for nine months, and I don't need any more stretch marks. My bottles don't have rubber nipples on them and I can't even look at a rectal thermometer without flexing my cheeks together.

I wonder if she'd fall for the monkey-as-grandchild thing.

Why not? I'm already Italian and I could always say the father was Greek.

Where's the Toilet?

Nothing unusual happened when I opened the front door to the new house; everything looked the very same way it did when I left the night before after moving some more stuff in. It wasn't until I tried to find room on the kitchen counter to put my bottle of water down that I noticed that there was a more than enough room for me to put my bottle down.

Too much room.

The kind of room that was big enough to fit a CD player and our drill kit, which weren't on the kitchen counter anymore.

What? I said to myself—I don't get it. I don't understand. Where's my stuff?

"Honey," I said as I almost asked him if he had come the night before and taken the stereo in secret-- "We've been robbed."

I ran into the living room where I had put my new power saw, which I had bought only the day before, and saw a huge, gaping black hole where the saw had been.

I turned to look for the sander.

Gone.

The router.

Gone.

The chainsaw, my portable radio, my CDs—they stole Billie Holiday?—my husband's watch, and our new pedestal bathroom sink, still in the box from Home Depot, some of our wedding gifts, all gone.

GONE.

"Didn't you lock the door when you left?" my husband shouted, and I had, I knew that I had. "The back door is open!"

"I didn't leave it open," I said as I entered the backyard, and turned to see that it wouldn't have mattered if I locked the back door or not. The bedroom window and sash was smashed and pried open with a crowbar, still sitting stupidly on the windowsill.

Sons of bitches, I thought, you bastards. How dare you come into my house—a house I haven't even finished moving into yet--and steal my things. My personal stuff. What the hell are you going to do with a bathroom sink?

"What's that?" my husband said, pointing to a pile underneath the window.

And as I looked at it I felt hate, a kind of hate that couldn't have been purer than the belch of the Devil himself, because underneath the window that the thief had destroyed to get into my house and then steal its contents, was a present.

It was a big, fat pile of doody.

"He apparently eats well," my husband commented.

"Too bad we didn't have any porridge for him," I mentioned. "I'm calling the police! We'll get him! Now we have his DNA!"

So I called the police, who assured me that a detective and a fingerprint squad would be dispatched within the hour, although a genetic poop test was not currently available. As I listed off the items that were gone, I noticed that a big, empty moving box that I had also brought over the day before was missing, and realized that the bastards had used my own box to pack my things in when they were robbing me.

I went and stood on the front porch, waiting for the police and watching people that drove by. I gave them all mean looks in case one of them was the burglar with my bathroom sink in the trunk of his rusted '78 Monte Carlo.

I wanted to know where my stuff was, who had it and what the robber got for it. Did he buy a vial of crack with the money he got for my Billie Holiday CDs (not that she'd mind, but still), was he stuffing his face with food he bought with the money from my saw, making sure he had enough in him to leave his trademark turd at the house he was going to rob tonight?

What did the Turd Robber look like, I wondered. How long had he been watching our house? What else did he know about us? I wanted to call his mother, tell her what her son did and then make her come over to clean up the pile. You raised an animal, I wanted to tell her, YOU DID NOT DO A SATISFACTORY JOB AS A PARENT!

I work 25 eight-hour days to make the equivalent to what the Turd Robber took from us, and I'll work twenty-two more to pay for the new alarm system, wrought iron bars on the windows and our new baby Doberman. It probably took him 10-15 minutes to wipe out my possessions, my window, and most of all, my sense of security.

Thirteen hours after we initially made our report, a police guy showed up. There was no detective, no squad, just a guy in black with a lunchbox full of powder and some blush brushes. All he raised were the oily rubbings of the Turd Robber's nose against the window and the side of his palm, and then just flat out refused to even look at the pile.

I wondered what I had done to get karma back like this. I'm generally a good person, I think--I yield to other cars in traffic, slow down for school zones, will not spread rumors without proof of partial truth, and only hate two people on the entire face of the planet, one of which doesn't even live here anymore.

After the police guy left, I secured the window as best as I could, and thought about what it took for one person to steal from another, to enter their home and rifle through their life. For someone to easily destroy somebody else's property because they were too lazy to get a job, or get a job and then embezzle. Was his family hungry? Where they sleeping underneath a freeway overpass?

What would drive a person to steal from someone else, then take a shit underneath their bedroom window?

None of the above, I finally decided, as the window was as shut as it was going to get, and I prayed that it didn't rain.

None of the above, it was plain and simple.

All it really took was an asshole.

The Egg Doesn't Fall Far From the Ovary

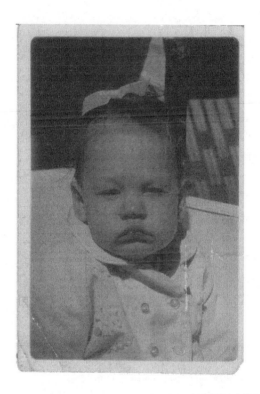

She was never one to mince her words.

Three seconds after I was born, a dutiful nurse leaned over her and asked quietly, "Do you want to know what you had, Mrs. Notaro?"

"I don't give a damn if I just gave birth to a monkey," she shot back. "*Somebody* get me a cigarette."

She's my mother. She's always been my mother. She'll always be my mother. She's a mother of many talents.

When I was in grade school and she heard the password phrase "*Mom, tell her to stop touching meee!*" she amazed all three of her daughters by possessing the ability to drive a Country Squire station wagon with one hand while simultaneously smacking the crap out of us with her flip-flop in the other without ever taking her eyes off the road. Not even our school bus driver could do that. She could also go into the bathroom, close the door, wiggle her nose and come out with a brand new hair color. Samantha wasn't that brave. She knew exactly when Santa was going to come on Christmas Eve, and always ushered us outside with our grandfather just in time. Other families with talentless mothers had to wait all night long for their presents. I've even heard her exact her biting, yet hysterical wit on occasion, like the moment when she suddenly quipped, "The only taste that girl has is in her mouth," while at a baby shower some years ago.

As children, we were pretty impressed. As an adult, I am stupefied. Although I realize that Miss Clairol was the magic, the flip-flop thing is still impossible, but what's truly the clincher is that by the time she was twenty-seven, she had three little girls. *Three kids.* Three other mouthy human beings to dress, feed and wipe. I'm thirty and I only have a dog, which I forget to feed at least three times a week, a dependent with whom I'm not ever required to complete the last step in the potty experience.

There's no way I could do it. I don't think my mother had time to cut her toenails until one day when she was in her mid-forties and my youngest sister drove away to college. By that time, she had rivaled anything that was created biologically by Howard Hughes and had also taken to wearing clown shoes. She was too busy mopping the kitchen floor every morning to indulge herself in such frivolous pampering. Her only extraneous and fun hobbies were smoking and the taking of aspirin to combat the headache that she got in 1972 that just never went away, and when Tylenol was invented, well, it rivaled anything that Prozac could claim.

When she was very pregnant with my sister, Lisa, I was in kindergarten and took my first school bus ride. Naturally, on the return trip that afternoon, the bus rear-ended another car, and of course, I was the only kid to get hurt. As my eye began to swell and discolor, the driver anxiously sped his way to my stop, though before he could get me off the bus I threw up right next to him (I was a very nervous child). I flew down the steps to my mother, identified as The Big Belly, and I clutched her leg, sobbing hysterically. I was safe. I was okay. My black eye, now puffed up so big I couldn't even open it, wasn't even that bad. My mom would protect and save me. I was going to *live*.

That is, until she began to pry and peel me off her leg with both hands, saying, "Little girl, um, stop it. Control yourself, little girl. Um, would somebody please help me?" and I looked up at The Big Belly until I could see over it, or at least enough to identify the belly as somebody I had never seen before. She wasn't my mother. It wasn't even my stop.

The bus driver, now thoroughly disgusted, led me back on the bus, where I threw up one more time. When we arrived at my real stop, he handed me over to the True Big Belly, who was horrified at my quivering, swollen, hyperventilating, vomit-splashed state, bellowing over and over again, "That wasn't my mother! Where is my mommy! Who is my mommy!" Doing what any good mother would, she lit a cigarette, piled me into to the Country Squire, drove back to the school and promptly got that bus driver fired. Then we went back home and she put ice on my head, though to this day one of my eyes is smaller than the other.

I was remembering that incident while we were watching a tape of Lisa's ultrasound yesterday, as my nephew, who will be born right around Mother's Day, twisted and turned in my sister's own Big Belly. Through the fuzz of the gray and black shadows and static, we watched and he moved his little fist, then turned towards us directly so we could fully see his face, and yawned.

"Oh my God, this is unreal. *Unreal*," my mother said, mesmerized by the sight of her first grandchild. "I can't believe it, it's just unreal. Too much."

If I didn't know better, I thought I saw her quickly reach for her pack of cigarettes, and then suddenly stop when she remembered.

She doesn't smoke anymore. She gave it up, cold turkey, when she found out that she was going to be a Nana.

"I'll be damned if that baby gets close enough to any smoke that he can even see it," I've heard her say.

Sometimes, I don't even think she misses it.

We watched the rest of the tape, as we previewed that kid's arms, legs, toes and naughty bits, and wondered aloud if his nose was really going to be that big.

When it was over, my mother got up, shook her head, headed straight for the kitchen, shook out of the bottle and then swallowed two Tylenols.

Yep. She's my mother.

Raw Genius Material

I should have known better. I had been warned.

My friend Jamie told me that I shouldn't have confessed to my husband.

"If you tell him, he has no choice but to be jealous," she said over the phone. "He'll never let you live it down, and he'll never forget or forgive you. He'll want revenge, and he'll go and do the same thing, but he'll try to out do you. Don't tell him, let it be a secret you keep until you *die*."

She was speaking from experience. She had already known what would happen, had lived through it with her own husband.

"He'll never be able to trust you again, that is, if you guys even stay together," she urged over the receiver. "And he'll throw it in your face every time you have an argument. Believe me, it was a mistake I'll never make again."

But when my husband came home that night, I tried to contain myself and act as if everything was normal, but I'm a very bad actress and an even worse liar.

"You bought me flowers?" he said with a puzzled look as I held them out. "And chocolate? I hate chocolate. Please tell me that gold spandex thing with the lace on it is for you, because the last time we went through this, you said I looked like Liberace and I wasn't allowed to touch you for months."

"Look," I tried to say excitedly as I held the garment up. "It has bells on it!"

"Haven't you toyed with my masculinity enough?" he cried, and then he gasped. "Oh my God. You've cheated!"

"I DID NOT!!" I blurted out.

"Who is it?" he demanded. "The meter reader? The mailman? One of those convicts that sends you letters?"

"What?" I said, a little bit puzzled. "I'm not having an affair! I'm a *genius*, I'll have you know, and I did NOT cheat!"

"Honey, I'm sorry, but you're not a genius," he said as he took off his coat. "I can see right through you, especially when you're holding up the gold, lacy thing!"

"I am SO a genius!" I pouted. "I knew it! Jamie *said* you'd act this way! I took the test and it's true. My brain should be put in a jar and examined, I'm so smart!"

"What test?" he asked. "And we've already had your head examined and it didn't do much good! I can tell you're STILL picking at your face, you know."

"Geniuses have a lot on their minds," I replied. "I have to have an outlet for my smart tension, I have the whole world to worry about now. They're all looking to me for answers! I took a test on the Internet and I could be a member of MENSES."

He just looked at me. "Oh, I think you already are," he said laughing. "Where's this test? I want to see it."

"No you don't!" I said, running into the office to block the keyboard. "Jamie said you'd do this. She said you'd be jealous of my...geniusocity!"

"If you're so smart," my husband said. "What's four plus two divided by nine? Seven? Four? None?"

"Jamie said you would resent me and my brain!" I quipped. "I should have just kept my geniusness a secret like she said!"

"Why did she say that?" he asked me, and then he smiled. "Oh, let me guess. Because....maybe....*she's a genius, too?*"

"Why, yes she is," I nodded. "And when she took that test and told her husband, it caused all kinds of trouble and he got all mad because he took the test and he's not a genius. He's just ordinary folk."

"I'm taking that test," he said, trying to push me out of the way.

"No, honey, don't!" I said. "It could only hurt you, and I'm perfectly fine that I married beneath my intelligencia."

"You're not a genius," he said, pushing me aside.

"I'm trying to understand your feelings, honey, I really am," I tried to say in a soft tone. "But there's a gap here. My communicating with you is about the same as you communicating with....Bella. We're at different levels." And then I moved my hands up and down for emphasis, a visual demonstration my average husband could comprehend.

"Bella, our *dog*?" my husband said as he looked at her, her little doggie body all contorted into a ball as she tried to eat her own foot.

"You're just not one of my cognitive brethren," I suggested. "Your brow is too pronounced."

"Well, then, go in the living room and split an atom or something," he said as he shooed me away. "I'm taking this test and if you leave me alone, I'll kill a carrot for dinner with my spear and a big rock when I'm done."

"Jealousy is such a primitive emotion," I said as I left.

In five minutes, I heard him calling me.

"What did you put for this one: Plant is to Seed as Human is to: ovary, sperm, ovum, uterus, or embryo?" he yelled.

I thought about it for a minute, and walked into the office.

"Oh yeah," I said nodding my head. "Whatever 'C' was."

"I'm gonna put 'embryo,'" he said, clicking the mouse.

"If that's 'C,' that's right!" I agreed.

"And what about, 'If you rearrange the letters LIGARAE, you would have the name of a river, country, city, animal or plant?" he wondered.

"Um, 'C,'" I said again.

"And 'What would be the next number in this series? 2...3...5 —"

"'C'!" I said.

"Did you pick 'C' for every question?" he asked me.

I smiled. "'C' is always the answer," I said, letting him in on the secret. "Pretty genius, huh? I learned that the fifth time I took the SAT's!"

"Um, what exactly was your IQ score?" he asked, and I reached over and picked up the proof I had printed out.

"Look at that! I'm so much more geniuser than the general population that I'm basically off the charts!" I pronounced as I showed him my results.

He looked at it for a minute. "Um, well," he stuttered. "Well, you're off the charts, all right, but honey, genius is over *here,* and your score is.....over *here.* According to this, you should be balled up on the floor with your foot in your mouth."

"What!" I shouted, snatching the paper from him. "I don't understand! You're kidding!"

"No, I'm not, it says it right here," my husband said as he smiled and began moving his hands up and down.

"Different levels," he whispered.

Don't Blame Fidel

My husband was flipping through the ASU class schedule a couple of weeks ago when I heard it.

"That sounds like a good class," I heard him say to himself. "Latin American History From the Dawn of Time."

My body immediately flew into alarm mode. I rushed into the living room where he sat.

"Oh, no," I protested, shaking my head. "Not a chance. You are NOT taking that class. I can't—*I won't*—live through that! Pick something else!"

Let me say right now that when my husband wanted to go back to college several years ago, I was all for it. All for it. I bought him a new backpack and went to Sears to buy him cool school clothes, everything my little student would need. But it was soon apparent during his first semester back that the wasn't the same kind of student I remembered being. He *read*. He did his homework. He joined study groups. He wrote his *own* papers. He went to his professor's office hours and talked about...*stuff.* I mean, I couldn't pick most of my college professors out of a line-up, and he was having *conversations* with them that didn't consist solely of academic disciplinary action!

I finally understood what kind of student my husband was when he discovered that, years ago, I had once had his current teacher for some English class.

"I think she's a very efficient lecturer, but to be honest, that thing she does with her face is a little distracting," he commented.

"What thing?" I asked. "She does something with her face?"

"How could you not notice?" he sighed. "She's an obsessive blinker. One time, I counted. She blinked 273 times in 60 seconds! Didn't that bother you?"

"I didn't notice it, but I sure couldn't see those things from the last row," I chuckled. "Your eyes must be sharp!"

My husband looked away very quickly and began studying the point of his pencil.

"Wait a minute," I said. "Where do you sit in class?"

"In a chair," he mumbled quickly.

"Oh no!" I screamed, horrified. "You're a first-rower! You sit in the first row! Oh my God. I bet you ask questions, too! And you VOLUNTEER, don't you? If you say that you have actively engaged in a heated debate that extended past the ringing of the bell, I am leaving you!"

He just looked at the floor in shame.

It was true. My husband was a teacher's pet, but not with just one teacher. He sucked up to ALL of them.   In fact, his appetite for education was not limited to the classroom.

Soon, he wanted to discuss things he was learning, predominately when I was watching TV.

"*Richard III* is a very interesting play," he mentioned once when I was watching *Will and Grace*. "Let's act out a scene! This will be so much fun! I'll be Richard! 'Now is the winter of our discontent....'"

When he enrolled in History of Foreign Affairs, my husband could talk about nothing else.

"Now, really," he asked one night when I was watching *Law and Order*. "In 1965, when the United States intervened in the Dominican Republic revolution, was it to protect American lives or was it a justification to prevent a Castroite regime?"

"I don't know, Good Will Hunting," I said. "I was an embryo. Would you not talk over Lenny, please? I think he's been drinking again."

When he began taking Spanish, our TV set was only allowed to be on the Telemundo channel so my husband could reinforce his classwork by watching Spanish soap operas.

"I can't believe Carmelita left Jose and now is marrying Pedro!" he shouted in a fury one night as we were getting ready for bed. "He tried to poison her whole family last week, you know! He mixed battery acid into the mole! Jose ate it and it burned off his lips! His lips are gone! *No tiene labios!*"

Last semester, he was completely immersed in his The Bible as Literature class, developed an odd dialect, and would not hesitate to interrupt Must-See TV to burst into scripture.

"Brothers-ah and Sisters-ah," he said to no one, "Thou shall not-ah kill-ah! Thou shall not-ah steal-ah! Honor your fath-ah and moth-ah!"

"You sound like an old Italian lady from Brooklyn," I said.

"DAY-MON! DAY-MON!" my husband shouted.

I leaned over and punched him in the arm.

"Wow," I said. "Look, the Lord works fast! It's forming a bruise already!"

So you see, Latin American History was completely out of the question. I had decided that as long as I was being forced to live through the classes with my husband, they might as well be something that I would enjoy.

"Why can't you enroll in 'Gazebo and Hot Tub Construction 101' or 'Introduction to Sprinkler Installation'?" I begged. "Take something like that. Besides, haven't you already taken Latin American History? I'm sure you did; I remember one semester when you wore nothing but fatigues, grew that scraggly beard, started smoking cigars and insisted on being called 'comrade'!"

"That was History of Cuba!" he replied. "Besides, I thought you were supposed to be supportive of my education!"

"I bought you that beret!" I shouted. "And I was tolerant when every time you spoke a sentence, you had to put one foot up on a chair, cross your arms and point at somebody!"

"But I need to take this class to graduate next semester!" my husband pouted.

I thought about it. "Okay, fine," I finally said. "Latin American History is fine, I guess I can handle the torture for one more semester. Go ahead and take it. But don't get any big ideas about growing cocaine in the backyard!"

"I won't, I promise," he said, smiling. "And guess what? Did I mention I've decided to go to graduate school?"

Page, Plant and the Little Guy

My friend Jamie's ex-boyfriend never liked me.

Once he even asked Jamie if I wore a wig because what was on my head didn't appear to him like the hair of a human.

As it happens, her ex-boyfriend accused me of being a witch and casting a hurtful hex on him because, since they broke up, his entire life blew up like a thousand pounds of fertilizer. Which is what I thought he was, anyway.

Because they had parted ways, he retained the tickets to the Page & Plant show as terms of the dissociation, even though he was never really sure who Led Zeppelin was, and this left her dream of seeing the mighty legends live one last time, dead before she even woke up.

So I wiggled my nose a couple of times, and I got a Fed Ex package in the mail with two Page & Plant tickets in it.

I bestowed these to Jamie, but there was one problem.

A long time ago, when we were in seventh grade, we went to a dance, the one and only dance we ever went to. Jamie was haunted by a short boy who had, judging by his aroma, bathed in a boiling vat of Brüt and had smoked several cigars. He chased her all night, *all night,* until he begged her so shamefully when "Stairway to Heaven" was played that she considered it charity and said OK. He held her tight. Then he popped a boner. It is a very long song. She now has flashbacks. It's something that torments her.

"What if they play 'Stairway to Heaven' and I can't get away from it?" she asked.

I told her not to worry about it. I was sure that Robert and Jimmy were probably pretty embarrassed of that song by now and, unlike the Glenn Frey and Don Henley, who abandoned all their Eagles pride by releasing of "Boys of

Summer" and "Smuggler's Blues," they'd rather drink gas that play it.

Anyway, we had other issues.

"Remember," I told her. "When we go to the show, dress like you're from Sunnyslope."

But when we got there, I wasn't at all prepared. Did you know that they still make ankle boots with fringe on them, and that tube tops are still alive and thrashing in certain parts of this city? I didn't. I thought for sure that elastic had some sort of expiration date, or a tag inside of the tube top that was stamped "Best if used by 1978." We were the only women in the whole damn arena wearing *bras*.

"Somebody needs to tell these people that even Stevie Nicks doesn't wear gauze anymore unless she has a scabby wound," Jamie said.

The first and by far most amazing creatures we saw were these two Amazon girls, way more than six feet tall, dressed exactly alike in red KUPD T-shirts, tighter-than-the-law black jeans and black boots complete with four-inch high heels.

Their hair was identical, feathered on one side and pulled up on the other; their make-up was also identical, deep wine lipstick and a shameful amount of poorly applied blue eyeliner. The closer we got, the more horrifying the apparition became, because the closer we got, the more apparent it became that these girls weren't just alike, they were the same. Exactly the same. So much the same that they had become one another, because you see, somewhere in the laboratories of Wrigley's Gum, some horrible accident had occurred, some genetic splicing gone unpleasantly wrong, and we were looking at the product.

"Those sure as hell aren't the Double Mint Twins," I whispered, mesmerized.

"Uh-uh," Jamie whispered back. "Them's the Big Red Twins."

Big Red was right. We were so spooked that we just kept walking, walked right past the section to our seats, not saying a word to each other, until I saw a man in a banana hat and a black see-through mesh half-shirt point to us and tell his friend, "See? I told ya. *There's* a couple of Hotties!"

Well, I've been called a lot of things in my life, some of them have even begun with an H, but I've never been called a "Hottie" by a man whose nipples I could reach out and pinch.

"Did you hear what he called us?" I said as I elbowed Jamie who, instead of responding, shrieked.

"Not again!" she cried.

And there, walking toward us, were the Big Red Twins.

"Oh my God," I realized, "They're walking the circuit. They're cruising!"

They passed by us, slinking and prowling, seeing and being seen.

Even the banana man looked.

We walked around one more time just to see the Twins but, as we returned to the place where we had spotted them earlier, we caught only a glimpse of something red with four legs slipping into a service elevator.

We decided to find our seats, which were amazingly good, directly off stage, 14 rows up and next to the stairs. We could see down into the backstage part, where all the equipment and roadies were.

That's when we saw an odd little foreign man in green shorts and argyle socks trying to squeeze his way backstage and, after a couple of ill-fated efforts, he finally succeeded.

He met up with a backstage guy who whispered to him, they both nodded, and they started making gestures with their hands as if they were measuring something, like a block of ice. The odd little man pulled something out of his back pocket and handed it to the backstage guy, and he took it.

We couldn't believe our good fortune. We were witnessing what could have possibly been a celebrity drug deal, and we couldn't take our eyes off it. We were hypnotized.

Until the little guy looked up and saw us.

"CAUGHT!" Jamie cried as she looked straight ahead. "He saw us! He saw us! Don't look over!"

Of course we did, and got caught five more times, and the last time we looked over, he was giving us the thumbs up.

We, cordially, responded the greeting. Thumbs up.

"I play bongos," he yelled up to us.

"That's nice," we yelled back.

"I play bongos for Led Zeppelin," he insisted.

"Sure you do," I screamed back. "My dad's the singer. You can forget it, we're not going to have sex with you, little man."

Just then, the lights went down and Tragically Hip took the stage, and that was when the real fun began. It dark and everyone in the arena was piss drunk, and we had aisle seats next to the stairs, which meant that we got to see a bunch of people fall down. The more the night progressed, the harder they fell. And some just plain stayed down.

Except for one man. He stumbled down the stairs, beer in hand and more, much more, in his belly, looking for a place to call his own.

"Hey," he slurred, tapping the man seated behind us. "Move over. Move over there. Lemme sit down. I wanna sit here."

The man behind us stoutly refused and the beggar continued down the aisle until he tapped another man a couple of rows ahead of us. I saw as the man stood up, turned around, cocked his elbow and popped the beggar square in the jaw with a crack so loud I heard it over the band, so hard that the beggar man caught air as he was lifted off the ground and flew three rows back, spraying himself and everybody else with what was left in his beer.

People clapped.

The beggar man didn't get the hint. He stood up, and like the complete jackass he was, tried to shake hands with the man that had just busted his lip open. He probably thought that the punch was a manly way of kissing.

"Hey clown," the other vested man warned, "You come near me and I'll clock you again!"

"WHY?" the beggar man whined. "WHY? You're the one who spilled my beer! Is that fair, man? My BEER!"

He was about to get another kiss, this one puckered up to his nose, when security galloped down and took him away as he kicked and screamed and bucked.

That was when I noticed that Jimmy Page looked odd. He looked like my Pop Pop dressed up in my Nana's clothes, but his face was wide, as wide as my butt. I was staring at his face when I saw another face jumping up behind him, smiling widely and happily.

Thumb up!

"Jesus, Jamie!" I shouted. "The drug dealer's on stage! The drug dealer is on stage and he's got a bongo drum in his hand!"

"I know," she answered, "But your dad's having a little trouble with the high notes."

And there he was, our odd little man, dancing, playing and waving at everyone, singing along. For some reason, we were proud. We were really proud, especially when he had his little solo bongo drum part, when the camera captured that smiling little face and projected him across the three big screens above the stage. That was our guy!

He was having a great time, such a great time that after everybody left the stage, he remained, as if the thousands of people were clapping just for him.

Well, at least we were. We were clapping for him and for Page & Plant, who had the very good sense not make us climb the Stairway to Heaven.

The odd little man stayed, long after the rest of the stage had fallen dark, with the thunder of the crowd still roaring, looking out at them and smiling broadly, with his thumbs raised straight up towards the sky.

Calling Foul

Some people say that when Karma comes back
to get you, it returns ten-fold.

I hope not.

One day in 1988, I killed something.

It was a big, fat, dirty gray pigeon, sitting
square in the middle of Washington Street with
another bird.

I saw it as I was driving from about a hundred yards away, and I wasn't worried because I thought that like other regular birds, it would fly away as soon as my car got close enough.

But it didn't fly away. Instead, it just sat there, even when the other bird with it flapped its wings and got out of the way.

I honked my horn, but the bird didn't budge. I was the leader in a congested pack of cars headed straight for the stubborn foul, so there wasn't anywhere for me to swerve or change lanes or do anything.

I was getting pretty close. I honked again.

The bird simply turned and looked at me, its shiny black eyes meeting mine.

In a last ditch effort, I tried to position the car equally over the bird, so maybe it could just drive over it without hurting it any.

I did the best I could. After I passed over the bird, I looked in the rear view mirror and saw a thousand gray feathers fly up in a plume toward the sun.

It was a bad thing.

And, as if I didn't feel horrible enough, when I told two of my friends about it, they convicted me in seconds flat.

"That bird was probably deaf," my friend Jamie said. "You killed a handicapped bird."

"Did you know that pigeons mate for life?" my friend Jeff piped in. "That bird that was with it was probably the husband or wife, and you killed it's spouse right in front of it. I'll bet you've destroyed a whole pigeon family. You're lucky that birds can't sue."

A couple of days later, I swear the widowed bird paid me a visit.

I was sitting on a bench at ASU, working on a dialogue with two people I barely knew from my Italian class, and one of them was a boy that I had a huge crush on.

I knew damn well that I couldn't impress him with my language skills, because I didn't have any, but that didn't stop me.

I made him laugh at some stupid joke, and when he finally turned to look at me, a pinecone from the tree above us hit me on the head.

Well, I prayed it was a pinecone, but when I felt warmth and ooze, I knew different.

A bird had taken a shit on my head, and the cute boy had seen the entire thing. He laughed even harder at me than he did at my joke, and refused to help me get the feces out of my hair because he said that birds carry typhoid, rabies and cholera. He never spoke to me again.

Because of that incident, I thought my penance was done, completed, fulfilled. I was a fool. The defecation was only the first fold.

Just a couple of weeks ago, I heard a weird sound in my bathroom, a fluttering of some kind, but I ignored it. A windstorm was

285

blowing all around my street; even cleaned all of the trash out of my front yard, so figured it was just a vent rattling around.

Until my husband came into the kitchen and mentioned that he had heard something, too.

"I know, I know," I said. "It's just the wind."

"I don't think so," he added. "The wind doesn't chirp."

"It's the wind," I insisted.

"But the wind doesn't flap it's wings," he replied. "A bird has flown into the vent."

If the bird flew in, I figured, the bird could fly back out.

The next morning, however, we heard fluttering noise again, and the chirp, but the chirp was a little fainter.

I decided right then and there that if the bird had any intention of dying in my vent, it was very, very mistaken. The last thing I needed was a dead bird smell enveloping my house, although it would more than cover up the already present dirty house smell.

So that night after work, I held the ladder and my husband climbed on the roof, but the vent was welded shut and we didn't have a flashlight. The only choice we had was to wait until the next morning and pray that the bird didn't die. Whenever the bird remained quiet for periods longer than about twenty minutes or so,

I took a broom handle and hit the vent until it chirped again, just to make sure that it was still alive.

We climbed on the roof the next morning and beat the vent with a screw driver until it broke open, but because I have a pitched roof, the pipe leading to the bathroom was too deep for us to see anything. It was strictly apparent that the bird, even if it possessed unbirdly powers, could not fly itself out.

Our next plan of action was to get off the roof, but not before I noticed just how much dog poo was scattered all around the backyard. The amount of it was obscene, and it occurred to me that I was probably going to have to pay someone a lot of money to pick it all up.

I still had some tools from my wannabe lesbian days, so I took what I could find and headed for the bathroom in an attempt to rip the vent out of the ceiling.

Although I only made myself bleed once, I did it. The vent fan was old, greasy, and had what appeared to be several petrified farts stuck to it.

In any case, the vent was free, which meant the bird was free to fly the hell out of my house.

But it didn't. In fact, the bird had been in the vent so long that it had become used to it and refused to come out.

"Come out, bird," my husband and I sang in unison. "Come out."

The bird poked its head out of the vent hole. I screamed.

"It's a bat!" I yelled. "It's a bat! Kill it!"

"It's not a bat," he said.

"Birds don't have ears!" I answered.

"Bats don't have beaks," he replied. "Put on your glasses."

And when I did, I saw that the bat was a little brown sparrow with a little white spot on its head. It was just a baby, but it was smart enough to know that two, white, hairless screeching monsters equated to DANGER.

So we closed the bathroom door and stood in the bedroom like the jackasses we are, until after about ten minutes, we heard the bird hop out.

It was at this time that my husband decided that he had to rush off to work, so it became my sole duty to capture the bird and let it go. I decided that I needed gloves in case the bird wanted to peck at me, so I dug up one yellow rubber glove and one white garden glove.

I went in.

Right away, the bird freaked out and started flying everywhere, flying into the shower wall, into the light fixture, into the sink. That bird was flying around like it was drunk, but a very crafty drunk at that, because I couldn't catch it. It flew past my head from behind, hit me in the leg in a mad attempt for the shower and bounced off the mirror a couple of times. The bird was driving me crazy. After a very long time, I gave up.

What was I supposed to do?

I ripped up some bread and put a little bowl of water on the toilet seat, closed the bathroom door and I went to work.

Later that night when we got home, as soon as we opened the bathroom door, the bird got all crazy again. It had rested all day and ate all of the bread, so it was fueled up and ready to go, zipping all over the bathroom.

I gave my husband the gloves and he grabbed a towel. It was a given that the bird would crash into one of the shower walls and fall on the floor, like it had done six times in the last four minutes, so we waited.

The bird flew around some more, landed on a light bulb and stayed there until it burned itself, then zoomed into the shower where it proceeded to fly into the wall and fall on the ground. My husband crouched, and with one quick move, he tossed the towel over the bird and caught it, in a maneuver usually reserved for wild animals that are sedated first.

We scooped the towel up, ran through the house before the bird unleashed itself and opened the towel to free the bird and let it fly back to it's other birdie friends.

But that didn't happen. Faced with the promise of wide-open space, the bird refused to fly, and was completely happy sitting on the ground in front of my car, looking at us.

Oh no, I thought, I've seen that look before. This sparrow smells death on my car.

So I quit waving at the bird to get him to fly and just jumped up and down in front of it, screaming, "I've killed bigger birds than you!" until it finally caught some air, glided across the street and nestled into my neighbor Bob's tree.

Did I finally complete my penance? Maybe?

Nope.

The next morning when Corbett went to brush his teeth, we realized that parts of the bird were still with us. They were with us on the toothpaste, on our toothbrushes, in the sink, on my CD player, and naturally, of course, in my hairbrush.

That bat had shit a lot for something that hadn't eaten in two days.

Only eight more fowls to go.